THE
REAL PRESENCE

Traditional Anglican Theology of
the Eucharist
Understood via the
Writings and Examples
of William Laud, Richard Hooker,
Robert Bellarmine, Modern
Science, and Eastern Orthodoxy

The Fourth Book of the Praxeologion

By Reverend Canon Mike DellaVecchia
of
Traditional Anglican Church of America

Edited by
Dea. Lisa DellaVecchia

THE REAL PRESENCE: Traditional Anglican Theology of the Eucharist, Understood via the Writings and Examples of William Laud, Richard Hooker, Robert Bellarmine, Modern Science, and Eastern Orthodoxy. The Fourth Book of the Praxeologion.

Written by Bp. Mike DellaVecchia. Edited by Dea. Lisa DellaVecchia.

Appearing as the Spring/Summer, 2024 Quarterly Edition of: The Jeremiad Christian Homesteaders Gazette [Publisher] www.jeremiadchristianhomesteadersgazette.com

Authored and published by permission and under the guidance of Archbishop Rick Aaron Reid of Traditional Anglican Church of America

© Copyright, 2024 Mike DellaVecchia and Dea. Lisa DellaVecchia. All Rights Reserved. Printed in the United States of America.

ISBN: 979-8-9889300-7-5

For my precious wife, Lisa, who long ago brought me home to Jesus. And, for our angelic children, Gioia, Mikey, Milo, Dave, Benjamin, and James, whose sweetness exemplifies more than anything *anywhere* that God profoundly loves me.

Books by The Jeremiad Christian Homesteader's Gazette: Available through Amazon, Barnes & Noble, Abe's Books, and other sellers:

The Real Presence: Traditional Anglican Theology of the Eucharist Understood via the Writings and Examples of William Laud, Richard Hooker, Robert Bellarmine, Modern Science, and Eastern Orthodoxy; Praxeologion No. 4; Hardcover – July 31, 2024

Theotokos: A Via Media for Anglicans on the Subject of Mary; Praxeologion No. 3; Paperback – March 19, 2024

Un-Loved: The Life and Stories of Arthur Seftel: The Life and Stories of Arthur Seftel; Hardcover – December 3, 2023

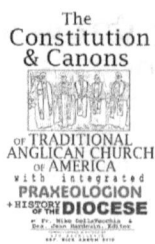

The Constitution & Canons of Traditional Anglican Church of America With Integrated Praxeologion (No. 1) and History of the Diocese; Hardcover – September 22, 2023

Ghost in the Brazen Bull: Using Continuing Anglican Theology to Confront the Ignominious Contraptions of the Artificial General Intelligence; Praxeologion No. 2; Paperback – September 22, 2023

Jeremiad Quarterly; Autumn 2023: Paperback

Table of Contents

FOREWARD i

CHAPTER 1: The Tale of the Permanently Interim Archbishop 1

CHAPTER 2: That God Is Perfect, but That Man Is Imperfect, Is Knowable 8

CHAPTER 3: Scripture, Tradition, & Reason, and Richard Hooker 19

CHAPTER 4: By Reference to the Orthodox *Metousiosis* as the More Catholic and Apophatic Theology of Transubstantiation 30

CHAPTER 5: The Struggles of William Laud as the Anglican Divine 34

CHAPTER 6: The Epiclesis & the Threefold Propitiation 47

CHAPTER 7: Fellowship & Ecclesiastical Concord Achieved Through the Eucharistic *Anamnesis* 51

CHAPTER 8: The Intention of the Priest, or Did It Matter Whatsoever Whether William Laud Was a Nice Person? 56

CHAPTER 9: Bringing Forward Richard Hooker's *Via Media* Eucharistic Theology 77

CHAPTER 10: Considering That the Contrite Laud Repented Just Before He Was Beheaded 81

CHAPTER 11: Using Irenaean Theodicy to Contemplate Whether Laud's Suffering on the Scaffold Was Sanctifying 85

CHAPTER 12: Fifty-One Years After Laud's Execution, Hooker's Real-Presence Theology Speaks Across Latitudes 88

CHAPTER 13: How the Sacramental Christian Participates in the Fullness of the Triune Godhead 94

CHAPTER 14: Aristotelian and Thomasian Hylomorphism Emboldens Attempts by the Lukewarm to Overlap Science & Metaphysics 140

CHAPTER 15: Conclusion 149

EPILOGUE: More About the Orthodox, but This Time, the Western Ones 152

APPENDIX A: The Bible is the True Source of the Traditional Anglican Mass — A Biblical Sacramental Reference Guide 162

APPENDIX B: Two Church Fathers Who Wrote About the Eucharist and Ecclesiology 233

FOREWARD

This book, *The Real Presence*, is a lesson that regards the way in which God associates Himself with the Bread and Wine during Holy Communion. It was written by an Anglican priest, whose Archbishop, a military veteran, had told him the following battlefield story, which will serve as the introduction for the rest of the book.

On Sunday, February 24, 1991, Holy Communion was celebrated by American troops stationed in Saudi Arabia, near the Iraqi border. The 210th Military Police Company, an Army National Guard Unit attached to the 101st active-duty Military Police, partook in Fellowship.

The Army was waiting for the command to begin the Ground War—the full-scale invasion of Iraq during Operation Desert Storm. Tension was heavy. Prayers were sent skyward. Saddam Hussein had brought to the breech over a million soldiers and, at 5,500, nearly double the number of Coalition tanks (*Cradle of Conflict: Iraq and the Birth of Modern U.S. Military Power;* Michael Knights; p. 20; United States Naval Institute: 2005).

That morning, Military Police Officer Rick Aaron Reid shared the Bread and Wine with the soldiers. They were partaking of uniquely consecrated rations from their units' ready-to-eat kits. They ate crackers

FOREWARD

and drank Kool-Aid in place of unleavened wafers and wine. The Gulf War was a Coalition victory, of course.

"Later on, folks said it was not really Holy Communion because it wasn't wine," remembered Reid, 33 years later. But these military communicants knew Christ was received.

Promoted later to First Sergeant, and later on elected in 2020 as the Archbishop of Traditional Anglican Church of America, Abp. Reid added, "Do you [not] think Christ understood?"

Patrolling more than 52 counties in the North Carolina Army National Guard, Abp. Reid was also the Field Manager for his state's Department of Agriculture (NC-AGR). If you were breaking the law near your barracks, or you were sneaking suspicious contraband illegally across municipal boundaries, you were brought to justice lickety-split as soon Reid and his team caught up with you. As an Army cop, he had endured a tougher boot camp than most soldiers. With face camouflage on at age 38 in the Gulf, he could frighten a tiger. Abp. Reid retired from the National Guard in 2010 at age 58.

FOREWARD

A lay Christian in 1991, he and his men affirmed that "Jesus was the authority," the ultimate Eucharistic consecrator, the undeniably present Son of God, Who had presided over that battlefield Mass. The soldiers wanted the Body and Blood, and God never disappoints such a Hope (Roman 5:5). The military had been slowly advancing toward the Iraqi border for 90 days and would be present in Iraq during one of the largest tank battles in history. The future Archbishop said, "Special times call for special actions in the desert."

The Iraqi Army was already bombarding the invaders with heavy artillery and manic foot-soldier attacks. After Kuwait was liberated an intense four days later, it would be another 90-day stretch for Abp. Reid. The men secured the region.

By the time of his retirement at age 65 from NC-AGR in 2017, Abp. Reid had received a Master of Divinity that focused on Theology from Emmanuel Baptist University, and later in 2005 a Doctorate in Christian Counseling from Jesus World Bible College. A seasoned organizer, he now built strong friendships with other upright religious men. Seeing that they had God at the top of their chain of command and had raised fine families, Abp. Reid co-consecrated Fr. Paul Leeman—who

FOREWARD

was himself a legendary Army engineer, and Fr. David Fleming, the founder of a shipping business. His chancery was buttressed by solid scholars, fluent in Ecclesiastical Latin, Masoretic Hebrew, and Koine Greek, such as Bishops Kenneth Walsh and Don Nozawa.

The message of Faith was clear in this bi-vocational Episcopate of businessmen, soldiers, and academics: If Christ said so, then we'll make it so! Parishioners knelt at attention during the *anaphora*!

The purpose of this book is to explain that Faith is the truly discernible means of invoking the Real Presence of God at the Christian altar. Christ Himself is the consecrator of the Bread and Wine.

Various liturgical elements such as the Eucharistic Prayer, the *anamnesis*, and the *epiclesis* will be taught in these pages. An exploration of beliefs concerning the Host (Consubstantiation, Transubstantiation, *metousiosis*) will consider at length how the Triune Godhead is thought to be invested in the Bread and Wine among the various churches and Christian Faith Traditions.

Moreover, analyses by theologians such as William Laud and Richard Hooker will be accompanied by pertinent historical

FOREWARD

information. Illustrations have been added to aid student comprehension.

More than anything else, the liturgical collaboration of the Communicants and the Priest with God is exposited here as being the crucial vehicle of Faith by which at least two or three Christians can be assured that God is in the midst of them during the Mass (Matthew 18:20).

FOREWARD

CHAPTER 1: The Tale of the Permanently Interim Archbishop

"For the wisdom of this world is foolishness with God. For it is written, He taketh the wise in their own craftiness" (1 Corinthians 3:19).

One of the legends whispered in the vestries of Continuing Anglicanism is the grim tale of an aging Archbishop and his eccentric means of remaining in power. His inability to reverse his sudden loss of influence within his Diocese will begin a discussion in these pages of the ways in which the Real Presence of the Eucharist can be

CHAPTER 1: The Tale of the Permanently Interim Archbishop

rationally comprehended to involve Itself with the Christian altar during Holy Communion. As we consider several churches with differing ideas about the Eucharist's modality of Substantiation, we examine what is expedient and what is not.

It was when his longtime friend, the outgoing senior shepherd, suddenly abdicated because of illness that our first minister's tale begins. Because I know the antihero of this sendup, I will neither name him nor cite the legal cases in which he became bitterly ensconced so that I can protect his identity. Truly, I retain affection for him because he was and is a likeable person.

I spent many cheerful hours in his vestry talking about professional boxing; or landscaping the campsites in the local parks, where he was a semi-retired forest ranger; or my farm, where I fed my chickens and ducks—that is, when I had them (a story for another time!). I found him to be notably more enjoyable as an everyman than as the intellectual who paved his theological ideas into a buoyant aggregate of overall human charm. Surely Pliny the Elder worked on his methods of influencing Emperor Vespasian of Rome while cultivating the Assyrian apple tree!

Suffice it also to say that this story will initiate our study of the Real Presence by considering various real-life narratives of ministers who

CHAPTER 1: The Tale of the Permanently Interim Archbishop

probably should have enjoyed maintaining their loveable pedestrian personalities rather than attempting to upstage the Grace of God at the altar and in the *wheresoever* throughout their greater ecclesia.

So, let us first detail how this antihero and his allies made matters worse for their hagridden denomination by interpreting Common Law to allow them to supersede Canon Law so that their man would automatically fill the *vacante* seat.

The man was, beyond the humdrum, brilliant. He was the founder and editor-in-chief of a popular religious magazine; had ministered all-ages groups, baptized and married a multitude; and, thusly had done enough for his religion to restrain onlookers (at first) from believing that a self-promoting prelate had slowly become convinced that he was mentally equipped with the omnipresence of God such that he could defy the laws of nature in the following way: He was known for professing that he, through a fiat which he intended that the Anglo-Catholic priests of his church respectively shared with God and himself, and with all priests in the world whose religions teach priests how to do it, was regularly performing Transubstantiation at his altar.

A fistfight erupted between the factions at a Synod, but neither side fared very well. Eyes

CHAPTER 1: The Tale of the Permanently Interim Archbishop

were functioning well enough now for the bemused sheep to size up whether or not these men were just a bunch of hotheaded egoists. By the time that policemen were required to break up the Synod, the juggernaut and his slowly dwindling number of friends were fast being squeezed out or embarrassed away from the 10,000-member Archdiocese.

They also retired, or died, or just lost the urge to fight. Their moment to become the inner circle for the top shepherd was all but over. Now the saga had become a dirge about what it took to make their champion finally give up.

Our discussion will eventually remind the reader of William Laud, the Anglican Divine, but it will be explained that while that master of Canterbury finally acquiesced to the English Parliament, along with giving a sorrowfully touching prayer requesting Redemption just before his head was chopped off, the life of the Permanently Interim Archbishop in this story is not yet over.

As a decade passed, our Überprelate grew saddened by the surmounting disagreement over his patristics by his member churches. So one day, he shockingly traveled many miles to the Midwest Parish where the main dissenters had their hub. He found a master key to the door of what he had decided was their upstart pro-

CHAPTER 1: The Tale of the Permanently Interim Archbishop

Cathedral. Deliberating that he had proprietorship over the ecclesiastical property owned by the parties who were serving under him, he changed the locks on the building and took possession of all the contents of the church, including the files and checkbooks. He was finally forced to desist in his hostile takeover by state authorities, and he could not afford to pursue the matter further in court. He had become financially insolvent.

"Great is the Lord, and greatly to be praised; and His greatness is unsearchable" (Psalm 145:3).

CHAPTER 1: The Tale of the Permanently Interim Archbishop

Ten years earlier, during the prior coup, when he was not suffering from heart disease, he had assumed rump Episcopal authority over a Diocesan vote for who should replace the outgoing Archbishop, an American-Episcopal veteran who had just succumbed to a stroke. Unable to employ the veto (because he had no cathedral authority), the maverick protested, using a commoner's "nullification" of the election and filed a statutory claim as a civil plaintiff, charging that the Constitution and Canons did not have the legal authority to "inhibit" his claim because he believed he could prove that he was the most senior member of the Episcopate and automatically deserved to be "elected." He settled for the title, "Interim Archbishop," which he retained for years, but was never eventually formally voted out of office.

Soon enough, this individual—who believed he could prove principles that were impossible to be rationally believed—was abandoned by his colleagues and allies and remanded himself to the rectorship of his own local Parish while his estranged Diocese refiled its existence under a new charter and name, in order to resist any future coups by him. He permanently exiled himself in his Sanctuary, which had no heat in the winter, and operated all the controls of his Digital Hymnal at the altar on Sundays, where he

CHAPTER 1: The Tale of the Permanently Interim Archbishop

performed the craft that he, by his personal theology, had always claimed was Transubstantiation.

"*Lex orandi, lex credendi,*" the Latin axiom attributed to Saint Prosper of Aquitaine, means: "The law of praying is the law of believing."

But how can a man believe and pray about something that he knows cannot be known? What *can* a man know?

CHAPTER 2: That God Is Perfect, but That Man Is Imperfect, Is Knowable

Man can know that God's will is perfect, but that his own Free Will, despite all his pageantry and well-researched fanfare, is imperfect.

Just as a person can only truly know his own thoughts and sins but not those of others, he does, however, know immeasurably more about God than he knows about anyone else, which is that God's universal salvific will is always ascertainable as being true. Truly, very few other matters involving church life should be contended as being "justified true belief" other than that we are each a sinner, but Christ is sinless. Truly, then:

> The heart is deceitful above all things, and desperately wicked: who can know it. (Jeremiah 17:9)?

In other words, because only perfection characterizes God, this makes God knowable in a

CHAPTER 2: That God Is Perfect, but That Man Is Imperfect, Is Knowable

huge way in which a man can never be known. That is, God is always singularly, infinitely perfect. However, man is imperfect in infinite ways.

And just as a man cannot know whether another person is ever intending to try to be perfect like God, he can eventually see and hear enough of a person's words and actions to apply Discernment as to whether he is trustworthy enough to be a friend. Grace is sufficient, as it influences Christians in Fellowship. However, human Free Will is seldom Godly.

As Saint Maximus the Confessor said about people, "So if it be a *Gnomic* will, it is derived from a *prior Gnomie* [God], and if it be so received, then that *Gnomie*, as the original form from which it is derived, is an essence [of God's will]" *(The Four Hundred Chapters on Love;* Saint Maximus the Confessor; Third Century; No. 77; A.D. 662).

Maximus meant that he, with man's *Gnomic* designation of Free Will, can at his very best *deliberate* on behalf of what he believes God Himself would decide. The term "Gnomie" derives from the Gr*eek gnome,* meaning *inclination* or *intention.* Since the ancient Church, it has been a theological concept signifying that a person's mind aspires to move

CHAPTER 2: That God Is Perfect, but That Man Is Imperfect, Is Knowable

spontaneously but correctly in making a good decision.

> Maximus: Do we choose for ourselves, voluntarily and deliberately? Or, involuntarily and without deliberation?
>
> Pyrrhus: Obviously, voluntarily and deliberately.
>
> Maximus: So then, the Gnomie is nothing else than an act of willing in a particular way, in relation to some real or assumed good. (*ibid*, No. 83-85)

Who or what kind of thinking, then, must be avoided? In the pages of this book, we list many such things as we beg the Creator, using the words our Savior taught us to pray in the Lord's Prayer, "And lead us not into temptation, but deliver us from evil" (Matthew 6:13).

Therefore, the Maverick Bishop in the above story should have prayed more than he consulted with his own psyche, and thus fought less against the dawn of his unpopularity.

CHAPTER 2: That God Is Perfect, but That Man Is Imperfect, Is Knowable

The Bishop Wars and the resultant two Civil Wars were extremely bloody, protracted conflicts arising from Archbishop Laud's sincere *intention* to preserve ritual purity at the altar (a success) despite his myopic intention to expedite church change (not immediately a success, and quite awful at first, actually).

Intention of the Priest: The Priest at the altar knows that he was taught, without any speck of his capacity for error stemming whatsoever from God, about Christ's perfect Sacrifice. Therefore, he knows that he must shed any doubt and believe in the purpose of his presidency at the altar, invoking the Real Presence of God sincerely to consecrate the Eucharist. He must be able to believe in what his discernment tells him is true. He is thus deliberating to share his intention with concrete purpose that the Holy

CHAPTER 2: *That God Is Perfect, but That Man Is Imperfect, Is Knowable*

Spirit wants for him, always that God will influence his human spirit to be faithful and good, so that he and his Communicants partaking of the bread can be saved. A good priest intends that prayerful self-depriving Love for the Church is better than his depending on the fallen world through the employment of his limited *Gnomic Free Will* to influence him for better.

Therefore, despite his human scarcity of (but still joyful) knowledge, he realizes that God's Grace is sufficient so that he can do all things through God, who strengthens him (Philippians 4:13).

The Intention of the Priest, as it interplays with the Matter and Form of the Eucharistic Liturgy, to consecrate, eat, and disburse the Eucharist, while exemplifying Grace, will be discussed more below in Chapter Eight, where it will be assessed whether Laud's reputation as a monstrous prelate should negate from posterity his credibility as a Eucharistic theologian and an Anglican ecclesiologist.

In the meantime, it is important to consider the Power of God, which, independent of the Intention of the Priest, will render Itself so discernible among the communicants that Its Grace cannot be resisted.

CHAPTER 2: *That God Is Perfect, but That Man Is Imperfect, Is Knowable*

To Dwell Among Them: Besides orienting the *anaphora* (that is, the Liturgy of the Word and the Eucharistic Prayer during Mass) that contains the *anamnesis* (that is, the Eternal Memory of the Eucharistic Prayer), along with the Oblation, and the *epiclesis* or Invocation of the Holy Spirit, and reading the Gospel, the Intention of the Priest is also to lead the Faithful in the Decalogue, the *Sursum corda,* the Nicene/Apostles Creed, the General Confession, the Prayer for Intentions, the Comfortable Words, the Doxology, the Thanksgiving prayer, the Exhortations, the Prayer for Humble Access, the *Agnus Dei,* and the *Gloria in Excelsis*; and to open and close the Mass.

A good priest intends to share his true Faith that the Lord is omnipresent, as proclaimed in biblical examples pertaining to God's Omnipresence (Psalms 139:7; Jeremiah 23:24).

The priest, who is the presider at Mass, yields to God in humility for "thy manifold and great mercy," kneeling before the *pleroma*, defined as God's "Fullness" (Colossians 1:9, 19; 25; 2:10; Matthew 1:22; 13:48; Acts 2:2, 28); and for His being so great that His presence deigns to oblige the appeals in which at least "two or three" witnesses are required to bear that Fullness of His Omnipresence in Fellowship. Chrysostom spoke thus about Hebrews 10:24-25:

CHAPTER 2: *That God Is Perfect, but That Man Is Imperfect, Is Knowable*

> What is, not forsaking the assembling of ourselves together? [1 Corinthians 7:29] He knew that much strength arises from being together and assembling together. For where two or three (it is said) are gathered together in My name, there am I in the midst of them [Matthew 18:20]; and again, That they may be One, as we also are [John 17:11]; and, They had all one heart and [one] soul. [Acts 4:32] And not this only, but also because love is increased by the gathering [of ourselves] together; and love being increased, of necessity the things of God must follow also. And earnest prayer (it is said) was made by the people [Acts 12:5] as the manner of some is. Here he not only exhorted, but also blamed [them]. (*Homily 19;* Saint John Chrysostom; Hebrews 10; Verses 24-25; d. A.D. 407).

The kinds of precious materials needed to construct a vessel mighty and graceful enough to contain the presence of God, that is, the Ark that once held the Ten Commandments, now are used to contain the bread of the Eucharist, which is why the Eucharist is not served in vessels made of paper, or clay, or plastic.

The term *Shekhinah* is the Hebrew word for the presence of God that "rests among" His prayerful people.

CHAPTER 2: That God Is Perfect, but That Man Is Imperfect, Is Knowable

> And let them make me a Sanctuary; that I may dwell among them (Exodus 25:8).

So powerful, however, was the sight of God's *Fullness* that in His mercy, God shielded Moses from it:

> And He said, Thou canst not see My Face: for there shall no man see Me, and live. ... And it shall come to pass, while my glory passeth by, that I will put thee in a clift of the rock, and will cover thee with my hand while I pass by. And I will take away mine hand, and thou shalt see my back parts: but my face shall not be seen. (Exodus 33:20, 22-23)

No one (besides Jesus) has ever been able to see God in his Fullness (John 1:18). But a portion "of His fullness we have all received, Grace for Grace" (John 1:15). The Beloved continue to be sanctified toward divinization through the Eucharist so that they can finally in the end witness this truth, that "when He shall appear, we shall be like Him; for we shall see Him as He is" (1 John 3:2-3).

Realizing that every jot and tittle of the Law (Matthew 5:18), with every one of its blessings and curses (Joshua 8:31-34), will be enforced upon Judgment Day, moves the thinker to consider that the Law is no longer being

CHAPTER 2: *That God Is Perfect, but That Man Is Imperfect, Is Knowable*

enforced by the Father on Earth, who had moved the hearts of men originally with signature earthquakes, stellar and lunar eclipses, and destruction of mountains (Job 9:5-6). That is, if there had never been a New Covenant, God would personally have gathered the unfaithful "like sheaves to the [threshing] floor" (Micah 4:12). However, a believer today grasps that God has dispensed such direct personal involvement with man in this present era: We will see it again, however, in the End of Days as described in Revelation.

Thus the Kingdom of Heaven, where milk and honey should have permanently flowed, will never occupy a place on the *current* Earth as a kind of restored Eden, neither within Jerusalem, nor anywhere in Canaan. Instead, the Son of Man, Who is invoked at the altar through the Eucharist, will cast into the Lake of Fire the goats and the tares, so that the sheep and the wheat— His Father's Elect—may enter the Kingdom of God, where the omnipotence of Christ shall issue forth the New Jerusalem (Matthew 25:31-46; Revelation 21, 22). "Thy Kingdom come, Thy Will be done, on Earth as it is in Heaven" is prayed for, just before the Eucharist is shared.

In the New Jerusalem, no divine thinning of the hordes needs to happen any longer: No longer will the Earth open up to swallow any Korah-like

CHAPTER 2: That God Is Perfect, but That Man Is Imperfect, Is Knowable

rebels (Numbers 16:32-34); no longer will there be a flood akin to that of Noah (Genesis 6-9); there will be no incineration of cities by the angels, similar to what happened to Sodom and Gomorrah (Genesis 19). This is because the Sacrifice by Christ is forever, "Blotting out the handwriting of ordinances that was against us, which was contrary to us, and took it out of the way, nailing it to His Cross" (Colossians 2:14).

When God's face is seeable by man as described at the end of the book of Revelation, man will no longer have the mortal ears that can deafen and transient hair to turn white. The Elect will instead be in their glorified bodies, resembling Him and seeing His Face, in *theosis*, knowing ultimate oneness with Him, "Who shall change our vile body, that it may be fashioned like unto his glorious body, according to the working whereby He is able even to subdue all things unto Himself" (Philippians 3:21).

But in the meantime, the largest amount of His *pleroma* and Omnipresence that man can withstand is divided among the Beloved, like a divine weight spread evenly over the joists' floor, together in Fellowship with God, before the altar, during Holy Communion.

But how can a priest say that he knows exactly *how* God would decide and do something? Should he profess that he knows just how God

CHAPTER 2: *That God Is Perfect, but That Man Is Imperfect, Is Knowable*

turns the bread the wine respectively into the Body and Blood? God forbid! Should he proclaim that God has given him the power to convert these gifts miraculously, through his human presence? Again, God forbid! Both presumptions would award man both the authority and power that God alone has. We would be better off to have the attitude of Job, who, after God revealed His Omnipotence to him, bewailed his own ignorance before God, saying:

> Who is he that hideth counsel without knowledge? therefore have I uttered that I understood not; things too wonderful for me, which I knew not...
>
> I have heard of thee by the hearing of the ear: but now mine eye seeth thee.
>
> Wherefore I abhor myself, and repent in dust and ashes. (Job 42:3, 5-6)

CHAPTER 3: Scripture, Tradition, & Reason, and Richard Hooker

For what man knoweth the things of a man, save the spirit of man which is in him? even so the things of God knoweth no man, but the Spirit of God. Now we have received, not the spirit of the world, but the spirit which is of God; that we might know the things that are freely given to us of God. Which things also we speak, not in the words which man's wisdom teacheth, but which the Holy Ghost teacheth; comparing spiritual things with spiritual.
(1 Corinthians 2:11-13)

CHAPTER 3: Scripture, Tradition, & Reason, and Richard Hooker

The Church must hold in tension **Scripture, Tradition, and Reason** (sometimes called the "three-legged stool of Anglicanism"). Each has equal authority and import. In this light, the phrase "*Lex orandi, lex credendi*" contends that it is in our rational worship that our belief in God, derived through good sense, retains its own psychological authority which is held in Communion with God, and throughout the Church. Richard Hooker is presumed by many to be the originator of the "stool" concept by way of the following teaching:

> What Scripture doth plainly deliver, to that the first place both of credit and obedience are due; the next whereunto, is what any man can necessarily conclude by force of Reason; after this, the voice of the Church succeedeth. That which the Church by her ecclesiastical authority shall probably think and define to be true or good, must in congruity of reason overrule all other inferior judgments whatsoever. (*On the Lawes of Ecclesiastical Politie*; Hooker, Richard; Book V; Chapter 8; Part 2; 1611)

Tradition, for instance, does not have a longer or thicker "leg" on the stool than that of Scripture or Reason, albeit certain denominations characterized by Apostolic Succession might hold the decretals by their Popes, Cardinals, or

CHAPTER 3: Scripture, Tradition, & Reason, and Richard Hooker

Bishops to be of higher credibility than they do the Gospel.

The ancient author of *De vocatione omnium gentium* (probably Saint Ambrose) predicated that Christendom must therefore be populated by believers, both clergy and laymen, if the concord of society is to be retained via the sound rational Bible-abiding Faithful:

> As to the law of supplication, thus the devotion of all the priests and all the faithful holds together, as if there were no one in any part of the world in which prayers of this kind are not celebrated by Christian peoples" / "Quam legem supplicationis ita omnium sacerdotum et omnium fidelium devotio concorditer tenet, ut nulla pars mundi sit, in qua hujusmodi orationes non celebrentur a populis Christianis (*De vocatione omnium gentium;* Book I; Chapter 12; Attr. Saint Ambrose of Milan; A.D. 397).

CHAPTER 3: Scripture, Tradition, & Reason, and Richard Hooker

Statue of Richard Hooker at Exeter Cathedra, in Devon, England.

Hooker, in discussing Article 25 of the Thirty-Nine Articles of Religion, further established that the Sacraments are not merely notes or the "signs and signifiers" that can be interpreted through fancy object lessons or contemporary rhetoric (as through modern Semiotics or Structuralism), but are effectual signs of Grace by which God works invisibly in the Faithful, who are held together in Fellowship, enjoying their sharing of the affinity of knowing that He is present (*ibid*, Hooker; Book V; Chapters 50-68). In terms of it being the human body described in 1 Corinthians 12:12-27, Hooker considers the *ecclesia* to be the womb of God wherein sound belief is gestated:

> The Church is to us that verie mother of our new birth in whose bowels wee are all bredd, at whose brestes wee receyve nourishment. As many therefore as are apparentlie to our judgment born of God,

CHAPTER 3: Scripture, Tradition, & Reason, and Richard Hooker

> they have the seede of theire regeneration by the ministerie of the Church, which useth to that ende and purpose not only the Word but the sacramentes, both havinge generative force and virtue. (*ibid*; Hooker; Book V; Chapter 50; Part 1; 1611)

Hesitancy to embrace the coequal aggregate of Scripture, Tradition, and Reason in embracing the Eucharist's Real Presence of Christ would allow confusion to metastasize into Church division, or schism. Confronted with the adulteries and litigiousness of Athenian Christians, Saint Paul of Tarsus preached that simplicity is the mode of instituting or explaining the Word:

> All things are lawful for me, but all things are not expedient: all things are lawful for me, but all things edify not. Let no man seek his own, but every man another's wealth. Whatsoever is sold in the shambles, that eat, asking no question for conscience sake: For the earth is the Lord's, and the fulness thereof. If any of them that believe not bid you to a feast, and ye be disposed to go; whatsoever is set before you, eat, asking no question for conscience sake. But if any man say unto you, this is offered in sacrifice unto idols, eat not for his sake that shewed it, and for conscience sake: for the earth is the Lord's,

CHAPTER 3: *Scripture, Tradition, & Reason, and Richard Hooker*

> and the fulness thereof: Conscience, I say, not thine own, but of the other: for why is my liberty judged of another man's conscience. (1 Corinthians 10:23-29)?

Hooker concurred with this principle on the subject of Holy Communion:

> Is there anything more expedite, clear, and easy, than that as Christ is termed our Life because through Him we obtain Life, so the parts of this Sacrament are his Body and Blood for that they are so to us who receiving them receive that ... which they are termed? The bread and cup are His body and blood because they are causes instrumental upon the receipt whereof the participation of his Body and Blood ensueth... [L]et our Lord's Apostle [Paul] be His interpreter: the bread is 'the Communion of' his Body and the wine is 'the Communion of' his Blood. The Real Presence of Christ's most blessed Body and Blood is not therefore to be sought for in the Sacrament, but in the worthy receiver of the Sacrament. (*ibid*, Hooker)

The Epistle referenced in the above excerpt from Hooker teaches:

> The cup of blessing which we bless, is it not the Communion of the blood of Christ? The bread which we break, is it not the

CHAPTER 3: Scripture, Tradition, & Reason, and Richard Hooker

> Communion of the Body of Christ? For we being many are one bread, and one body: for we are all partakers of that one bread. Behold Israel after the flesh: are not they which eat of the sacrifices partakers of the altar? What say I then? that the idol is any thing, or that which is offered in sacrifice to idols is any thing? But I say, that the things which the Gentiles sacrifice, they sacrifice to devils, and not to God: and I would not that ye should have fellowship with devils. Ye cannot drink the cup of the Lord, and the cup of devils: ye cannot be partakers of the Lord's table, and of the table of devils. (1 Corinthians 10:16-21)

Hooker continued, saying that the rituals and the ordinals do not have their own version of Grace in themselves, but merely are at God's disposal to be wrought, or not to be, as He chooses:

> As for the sacraments, they really exhibit, but for aught we can gather out of that which is written on them, they are not really nor do they really contain in themselves that Grace which with them or by them it pleaseth God to bestow... There is no sentence of Holy Scripture which saith that we cannot by this Sacrament be made partakers of His Body and Blood except they be first contained in the Sacrament, or the Sacrament converted

CHAPTER 3: Scripture, Tradition, & Reason, and Richard Hooker

> into them. 'This is my Body,' and 'This is my Blood,' being words of promise, [since] we all agree that by the Sacrament Christ doth really and truly in us perform His promise, why do we vainly trouble ourselves with so fierce contentions whether by consubstantiation, or else by Transubstantiation the Sacrament itself be first possessed with Christ, or no? (*ibid*, Hooker)

Does not God's Grace alone actualize the Sacrament?

As with Holy Communion, the other sacraments (e.g., Holy Baptism, Priestly Ordination, Holy Matrimony) have been blessed by God, Who, to His pleasure, allows the participation of His Church. Such a blessing, if not canonically conventional or valid from one church to another, is still licit for Anglicanism and most of Trinitarian churches with Apostolic Tradition if the Bishop allows convalidation of the sacrament involved (although being merely *licit* does not always denote the canonical validity within a church whose canon does not permit, for instance, a Roman Catholic or an Anglican to receive the Eucharist in an Eastern Orthodox church). The quality of executing a merely licit action is reserved for the allowance of, for example, an emergency baptism at the time of a person's imminent death by a layperson (i.e., in

CHAPTER 3: *Scripture, Tradition, & Reason, and Richard Hooker*

the complete absence of a priest or minister), or Last Rites given by a minister to an unrepentant mortal sinner when requested by a loved one. If the priest in being compelled to perform the Last Rites found himself without holy oil or holy water, prayer book, or Eucharist, the sacrament itself would still be licit, that is, blessed by God, just as the Sacrament of Reconciliation of the unbaptized thief on the cross in Luke 22:43 was valid, holy, licit, sound, and universally canonical because it was presided over by Christ the Savior, who endowed the Sacrament with His Grace, not man's. This same thief—it can never be forgotten—gained entrance into Paradise even without receiving a conventional Holy Baptism, indicating that God's direct Grace far surpasses any Grace that could be imparted through sacramental acts wrought with human hands. Because the thief was brought into the body of the Church by Christ's implied Baptism of Intention, the Intention of the Priest during Eucharistic Liturgy must also contain the same licit intention, one immediately inspired by Agape Love, as shown in these examples.

Hooker has thus impelled our credence further, urging us to abide the authority of Christ's being truly present during sacraments:

> A thing which no way can either further or hinder us howsoever it stand, because our participation of Christ in this Sacrament

CHAPTER 3: *Scripture, Tradition, & Reason, and Richard Hooker*

> dependeth on the cooperation of His omnipotent power which maketh it his Body and Blood to us, whether with change or without alteration of the elements such as they imagine, we need not greatly to care nor inquire. (*ibid*, Hooker)

The Bishops' Wars of 1639 and 1640 are discussed in this book (see Chapter 6) to present the case that one's interpretation of the Last Supper must always abide the mindset of Gospel peace, catholically shared by all in Communion, rather than allowing polemics to lead the Church into conflict:

> But all this language of disparagement of material sacrifices still leaves them on their own ground recognizing that the worship in spirit and in truth is not a mere inward and individual approach to God, but a corporate and therefore outward thing—a worship which publicly acknowledges God in all His gifts, though He needs them not; and a worship that finds central expression in the Eucharist, in which, according to the ordinance of Christ, bread and wine are presented to the Father, in the name of the Son, and in memorial of His passion, with the adoration and prayer and thanksgiving of sons, and blessed by the Holy Spirit to become the Lord's Body and Blood, and

partaken by the worshippers that they may be bound all together in Him. That was for the Christians the chief and central expression of rational service and bloodless sacrifice (*The Body of Christ: An Enquiry into the Institution and Doctrine of Holy Communion*; Charles Gore; p. 161; London: Murray, 1901).

CHAPTER 4: By Reference to the Orthodox *Metousiosis* as the More Catholic and Apophatic Theology of Transubstantiation

The Russian Orthodox Church, the Moscow Patriarchate, and the Western Rite churches, to their credit, do not rule on why a Christian must believe that God, via the priest, transforms the bread and wine into the Body and Blood, other than that, in taking the pertinent scriptural language literally, one is being acceptably faithful to the Word (Matthew 26:26-30; Mark 14:22-25; 1 Corinthians 11:23-25). *The Longer Catechism of the Eastern Orthodox Catholic Church* addresses the question in this way:

> **Question: 340.** How are we to understand the word, Transubstantiation?

CHAPTER 4: By Reference to the Orthodox Metousiosis *as the More Catholic and Apophatic Theology of Transubstantiation*

> **Answer:** In the exposition of the Faith by the Eastern Patriarchs, it is said that the word, Transubstantiation, is not to be taken to define the manner in which the bread and wine are changed into the Body and Blood of the Lord; for this none can understand but God; but only thus much is signified, that the bread truly, really, and substantially becomes the very true Body of the Lord, and the wine the very Blood of the Lord. (*The Longer Catechism of the Eastern Orthodox, Catholic Church*; Saint Philaret of Moscow; Question 340; Moscow; 1830)

The answer to the Transubstantiation question demonstrates the helpful use of Apophatic Theology; that is, it allows one's Faith to accept that one cannot know how something like this could possibly be true, permitting hopeful confidence nevertheless in the truth that Christ's Real Presence indeed involves Itself with the Body and Blood, even if it is unknowable *how*.

Just as it is taken at face value that God created the world from the Nihil, it is implied through sheer Faith that Christian beauty can be found in Negation Epistemology (i.e., understanding *more* by knowing *less*), thus closing the valve of vexatious exegetical worrying and just accepting that God, with His Word, created the world and

CHAPTER 4: By Reference to the Orthodox Metousiosis *as the More Catholic and Apophatic Theology of Transubstantiation*

all Life out of His profound omnibenevolent Love (Genesis 1-3; John 1).

Moreover, if a person were to contemplate touching the Tabernacle or Mount Sinai while God was occupying it, he could not know why, or by what "science," God knew the reverse-creational steps to make him instantly die for doing so (2 Samuel 6:1-7 and 1 Chronicles 13:9-12.; Exodus 19:12-13). For that matter, why or how God's voice is alternately incredibly loud or soft is never questioned but readily obliged (Job 37:2-12; 1 Kings 19:11-13). Thus, it is using Apophatic Theology (e.g., Additive Epistemology) to profess that it is sufficient that a worshiper can never know more than what God's Grace has gifted to human knowledge, the senses, and *a priori* and *a posteriori* reasoning as regards the Sacraments. It is a testament to God's Love that a believer can glorify in the infirmity of his seeing "through a glass, darkly" (1 Corinthians 13:12), and that Christian Faith is rendered more perfect in its intellectual and sensory weakness (2 Corinthians 12:9). That a believer's reliance on Hope that he can learn via inspiration, discernment, experience, and revelation only a jot of what God knows illustrates that the Father's Grace is nonetheless sufficient (2 Corinthians 12:9). Saint Philaret, addressing the subject of Holy Communion, added:

CHAPTER 4: *By Reference to the Orthodox* Metousiosis *as the More Catholic and Apophatic Theology of Transubstantiation*

In like manner John Damascene, treating of the Holy and Immaculate Mysteries of the Lord, writes thus: It is truly that Body, united with Godhead, which had its origin from the Holy Virgin; not as though that Body which ascended came down from heaven, but because the bread and wine themselves are changed into the Body and Blood of God. But if thou seekest after the manner how this is, let it suffice thee to be told that it is by the Holy Ghost; in like manner as, by the same Holy Ghost, the Lord formed flesh to himself, and in himself, from the Mother of God; nor know I aught more than this, that the Word of God is true, powerful, and almighty, but its manner of operation unsearchable. (*ibid*, Philaret; and, *The Fountain of Knowledge;* Saint John of Damascus; Book IV; Chapter 13; Sec. 7; A.D. 749)

CHAPTER 5: The Struggles of William Laud as the Anglican Divine

Image of Abp. William Laud, in stained glass, Cathedral of the Diocese of Chester, England.

William Laud, recognizing that the supernatural Hand of God was directly associating Itself with the Communion table, accepted the commission by King Charles I, the Catholic-leaning monarch who appointed him Archbishop of Canterbury, to write the *Book of Common Prayer* of 1637 and create a church polity as the inner circle of monarchical government. Laud's new Eucharistic Liturgy began the First Bishop's War (1639), which led to his impeachment in 1640, and the execution of himself and the King, in 1649 and 1654, respectively. His foes in his native Scotland, who were not obliging the Romish-

CHAPTER 5: The Struggles of Willam Laud as the Anglican Divine

sounding idea of the Real Presence, wanted to retain their Mass's metaphoric propitiation of Christ's Sacrifice, overseen by the Calvinist Covenanter government, rather than the Church of England.

To them, Laud's eye had set itself upon an imitation of the ancient clerical hierarchy, as evidenced by his insistence that Britain should adopt a formal Apostolic Succession, rather than the system of rule by bishops and presbyters who were substantiating their consecrations and elevations on purely biblical bases.

To Laud, however, it was instead valid to substantiate such consecrations in Episcopal Succession of one another—in the manner of Rome or Constantinople (with three Bishops doing the consecrating of one by the Laying of Hands)—but also squarely according to God's ancient promises.

Scriptural examples abound for an Episcopate and a Priesthood. First, there was the theophany of Melchizedek the Priest, who broke bread with Abraham as the first Elder-Patriarch of God's Chosen (Genesis 14:18-20). There was also the Creator's direct Covenant in oxen blood with the Elders of Israel in Exodus 24, and with Jacob, named by God as "Israel," in Genesis 35. These events in the Torah realized their Christian convalidation via the choosing of Christian

CHAPTER 5: The Struggles of Willam Laud as the Anglican Divine

Elders (equivalent to the office of Bishop), depicted in Acts 14:23.

It cannot be ignored that the Priesthood was instituted when, on Holy Thursday, Christ presided over the Last Supper and washed the feet of His Apostles, respectively telling them, to "do this in remembrance of Me" (Luke 22:19) and, exhorting, "For I have given you an example, that ye should do as I have done to you (John 13:14-15). Without these verses there could be no Apostolic Succession, nor could an Episcopate be formed without Christ's calling forward the profession by Simon Peter thrice that he loved Him and commanding Peter, "[Then] feed my lambs and sheep" (John 21:15-17).

With respect to calling any man a "Bishop," God has moral expectations of such men, and of deacons, to be upstanding, financially solvent, of sound repute, having only one wife, sober, et cetera (1 Timothy 3). However, as Laud would address it, an Ecclesiastical Polity must operate according to the gestalt of Scripture, Reason, and Tradition, as promulgated in his theology of the Eucharist.

This Euchology is found in a work called "A Relation of a Conference between William Laud, Lord Archbishop of Canterbury, and Mr. Fisher the Jesuit," which was originally published in 1639. In this Conference, Laud rejects the dogma

CHAPTER 5: The Struggles of Willam Laud as the Anglican Divine

of Transubstantiation. God alone knows what kind of "substantiation" is indeed taking place. The priest must simply present an ancient Form of the Invocation and Anamnesis, so that the Matter of a Substantiation can happen.

Laud, while Bishop of the Diocese of St. David's in Wales, exposited his theology of the Eucharist during this ecumenical debate against Roman Catholic polemics because he was commanded to do so by King James I. Confronting Laud's apologetics was the English Jesuit convert, Fr. John Percy (a.k.a. Mr. Fisher). Fisher was representing the aged Counter Reformationist, Society of Jesus scholar, Archbishop of Capua, Cardinal Robert Bellarmine.

Laud rejected the Catholic dogma of Transubstantiation on three principal grounds: That it was never spoken about by the Apostles, or by the Church or Desert Fathers; that it is not biblical; and that the dogma as predicated by Rome is not even Christian, because it is hardly rational (again, it fails at supporting Scripture, Tradition, and Reason). He said:

CHAPTER 5: The Struggles of Willam Laud as the Anglican Divine

> For Transubstantiation, first: That was never heard of in the primitive Church, nor till the Council of Lateran, nor can it be proved out of Scripture; and, taken properly, cannot stand with the grounds of Christian religion. *(A Relation of the Conference Between William Laud, Late Lord Archbishop of Canterbury, and Mr. Fisher the Jesuit, By Command of King James of Ever Blessed Memory*; Abp. William Laud; Conf. 1622; Publ. 1686; Sec. 33)

Apophatic theology.

Even the Eastern Orthodox Church, which straightly and sharply disagrees with Protestant views about the Eucharist, admitted that it would never presume to know the modality by which the bread and wine become the Body and Blood. Since the definitive 1672 Synod of

CHAPTER 5: The Struggles of Willam Laud as the Anglican Divine

Jerusalem, the Orthodox have referred to the process as "transmutation" or "change," which today they relate to as the unknowable *metousiosis*.

> Further, we believe that by the word 'transubstantiation' the manner is not explained, by which the bread and wine are changed into the Body and Blood of the Lord—for that is altogether incomprehensible and impossible, except by God Himself, and those who imagine to do so are involved in ignorance and impiety, but that the bread and the wine are after the consecration, not typically, nor figuratively, nor by superabundant Grace, nor by the communication or the presence of the Divinity alone of the Only begotten, transmuted into the Body and Blood of the Lord; neither is any accident of the bread, or of the wine, by any conversion or alteration, changed into any accident of the Body and Blood of Christ, but truly, and really, and substantially, doth the bread become the true Body Itself of the Lord, and the wine the Blood Itself of the Lord, as is said above. (*The Acts and Decrees of the Synod of Jerusalem: Sometimes Called the Council of Bethlehem: Holden under Dositheus, Patriarch of Jerusalem in 1672*; Transl. J.N.W.B. Robertson, Ed.; London, T, Baker: 1899)

CHAPTER 5: The Struggles of Willam Laud as the Anglican Divine

A priest, Roman or otherwise, presuming to be the agent whose own personal Grace helps produce the Transubstantiation instead of its being God acting solely by His invisible mystical means, would inadvertently be acting like a Gnostic magician if he contends that he can know that it is the result of his partnering with God that the bread and wine are converted at the altar. Indeed, no, Laud asserts, because only God acting by Himself could make such a change by His pleasure and can alone know whether He would deign to make such an event happen or when or how it happens.

> The Primitive Church never—nor did it dream—of a Transubstantiation, which the learned of the Roman party dare not understand properly, for a change of one substance into another, for then they must grant that Christ's real and true body is made of bread, and the bread that changed into it, which is properly Transubstantiation; nor yet can they express it in a credible way, as appears by Bellarmine's struggle about it, which yet in the end cannot be, or be called, Transubstantiation, and is that which at this day is a scandal to both Jew and

CHAPTER 5: The Struggles of Willam Laud as the Anglican Divine

Gentile, and the Church of God." (*ibid*, Laud; Sec. 38)

Bust of Cardinal Roberto Bellarmine, detail, in the Chiesa del Gesù, Rome.

To Bellarmine, the Sacrifice of the Mass has two essential parts: the Consecration (or blessing of the bread and wine by the priest), and the Communion (or consumption of the species). According to Bellarmine, the mystical change is begun firstly by the disappearing action of the bread, in the eating of the sacramental species by the Priest, who performs the "immolation" or "holocaust" of the sacrificial Victim by eating Him.

CHAPTER 5: The Struggles of Willam Laud as the Anglican Divine

However, according to Bellarmine, the holocaust is wholly supernatural, a mystical invisibility, that cannot happen without the Consecration by the cleric, a ritual akin to an Old Testament destruction of a lamb or dove in an altar sacrifice, which altogether signifies, to the Jesuit, that the destruction of the victim by the priest must be a real occurrence, as an ancient ritual executed by a Hebrew priest or patriarch: "Then Jacob offered sacrifice upon the mount [Gilead], and called his brethren to eat bread: and they did eat bread, and tarried all night in the mount" (Genesis 31:54). Bellarmine, calling to mind the burnt sacrifices of the herd in Leviticus 1 and 2, said:

> This is indeed proved, first of all, from the name of the sacrifice... Secondly, it is proved by practice of the Scriptures... And all the sacrifices that are called sacrifices in the Scriptures were necessarily to be made: if living, by killing; if inanimate solids, as the like, and salt, and incense, by combustion; if liquids, such as blood, wine, and water, by effusion: Leviticus 1 and 2. Nor is the example of Melchizedek inconsistent with these... (*Disputations about the Controversies of the Christian faith Against the Heretics of this Time: Three Volumes;* Abp. Robert Bellarmine, SJ, [Ingolstadt, 1586-1593; Paris, 1608], De

CHAPTER 5: The Struggles of Willam Laud as the Anglican Divine

missa, Vol. 1; Chapter XXVII; Table. III, Col. 792; Ingolstadt: 1586-1593; Paris: 1608)

Laud, like any Christian priest, and thus serving in the order of Melchizedek, would thereby only be breaking the bread of Fellowship, rather than killing an actual transmuted fleshly victim, as Christ Himself had already been "the propitiation for our sins" once and for all, as Laud cites 1 John 2:1-2 in the Comfortable Words. This language of his has been retained for the 1928 Liturgy of the *Book of Common Prayer* since his 1637 edition.

That is, the "holocaust" mentioned by Bellarmine as the presider's eating of the actually materialized victim, is replaced by Laud by the supernatural Substantiation of the Real Presence, a medium and a method that is necessarily impossible for any human to understand.

Neither the Orthodox, who believe in Transubstantiation (though not in the way that Roman Catholics do), nor Catholic-minded Anglicans such as Laud and King James I, would dare to pretend that bread's conversion into the flesh of Jesus has been *rendered by* one of their priests or that the priest would be in *command of* the conversion.

> The conversion of the bread and wine into the Body and Blood of Christ is substantial, but after a secret and effable manner, and

CHAPTER 5: The Struggles of Willam Laud as the Anglican Divine

> not like in all things to any natural conversion whatsoever. (*ibid*, Laud; Sec. 35)

Bellarmine contended that as eating the consecrated Eucharist is a prerequisite for Salvation, Christ's Body must come into the room of the bread by way of an action that is comparable to how a bicep muscle draws the arm toward the torso, as an "adductive conversion" of the bread, as one thing transposes itself with the volume of the other, the first being voided (*Trapp's Complete Commentary*; On Matthew 26:26; John Trapp; Oxford: 1649).

For Laud, it is not preposterous "to believe Transubstantiation is not simply necessary to Salvation. And yet [Bellarmine] knew well the Church had determined it. And Bellarmine, after an intricate, tedious, and almost inexplicable Discourse about an Adductive Conversion (a thing which neither Divinity, nor Philosophy ever heard of till then) is at last forced to come" (*ibid*, Laud; Sec. 35).

It seems, therefore, that Laud's chief objection to the doctrine of Transubstantiation is not that it argues that Christ is perceivably present. Rather it is that the Catholic dogma assigns a Tradition to the Real Presence by using only a literal translation of Scripture (i.e., "This is my body" and "This is my blood") that cannot be

CHAPTER 5: The Struggles of Willam Laud as the Anglican Divine

supported by Reason. Laud is content to say that Christ *is* nevertheless somehow present in or near or around the bread and wine, which is a significant admission, but he insists that the manner of the presence is mysterious, secret and ineffable. This matches the understanding of Consubstantiation confessed by Lutherans (*Real Presence Communion—Consubstantiation?;* Wisconsin Evangelical Lutheran Synod; WELS Topical Q&A. Waukesha, Wisconsin: 2008).

However, unlike the Lutherans, Laud is expressing that Transubstantiation is not impossible at the altar, but that it is knowable only to God, a case that should be referred to merely as the Real Presence that indwells the communicants upon their consumption of It. (The Orthodox, for their part, believe that *metousiosis* **always** happens, but that they are only collaborators and witnesses in this happenstance through the Invocation by their priest).

Instead of what Bellarmine referred to as "adduction," the method and type of conversion is a truth kept eternally ineffable by the Trinity alone, a factor that lands Laud's apophatic theology squarely in the psyche as a merely beautiful unsolvable mystery. Laud has no trouble accepting the "True Substantial Presence of Christ in the Eucharist" (*ibid*, Laud; Sec. 35). He simply does not excuse the voluble and

CHAPTER 5: The Struggles of Willam Laud as the Anglican Divine

imperious overreach regarding this sacred subject that only God can understand. He adds:

> Now if [Bellarmine] had left out Conversion, and affirmed only Christ's Real Presence there, after a mysterious, and indeed an ineffable manner, no man could have spoke better. (*ibid*, Laud; Sec. 35)

CHAPTER 6: The Epiclesis & the Threefold Propitiation

Epiclesis, *or Invocation, as Priest's hands are held above the bread and wine.*

On the question of Eucharistic Sacrifice, Laud argues that although the believer is blind to any perceivable kind of Conversion taking place on the altar, he participates in the Communion by necessity through the priest, who invokes God's Substantiation. The *epiclesis*—that is, the invoking of the Real Presence—occurs as the priest holds his hands above the bread and wine, and says, in Laud's 1637 Invocation:

> We most humbly beseech thee, and of thy almighty goodnesse vouchsafe so to blesse and sanctifie with thy word and holy Spirit

CHAPTER 6: The Epiclesis & the Threefold Propitiation

> these thy gifts and creatures of bread and wine, that they may bee unto us the body and bloud of thy most dearly beloved Son; so that wee receiving them according to thy Sonne our Saviour Jesus Christs holy institution, in remembrance of his death and passion, may be partakers of the same his most precious body and bloud.

Laud, in his contest with Fr. Percy, beautifully describes the Threefold Propitiation happening at the altar, which he identifies as (1) a supernatural sacrifice with the Real Presence; (2) Communion with others and God in creating the extraordinary Fellowship of Ecclesiastical Polity centered in the Church,[1] and (3) the individual sacrifice of the self to God:

> As Christ offered Himself up once for all, a full and all-sufficient sacrifice for the sin of the whole world, so did He institute and command a memory of this sacrifice in a Sacrament, even till His coming again. For, at the end of the Eucharist we offer up to God three sacrifices: One by the priest only, that is, the commemorative sacrifice of Christ's death, represented in the bread broken and wine poured out. Another by

---

[1] This is the Ecclesiastical Communion or Fellowship, where the Christian version of the Aristotelian "concord" is achieved as the Ecclesiastical Polity of the church (see Chapter 7).

CHAPTER 6: The Epiclesis & the Threefold Propitiation

> the priest and the people, jointly; and that is the Sacrifice of Praise and Thanksgiving, for all the Benefits and Graces we receive by the precious death of Christ. The third, by every particular man for himself only; and that is the Sacrifice of every man's body, and soul, to serve Him in both, all the rest of his life, for this blessing thus bestowed on him. (*ibid*, Laud; Sec. 35)

Thus, if there is indeed a holocaust on some existential plane of the actual invisible human flesh of Christ, or God's presence is otherwise merely consubstantially located, it is nonetheless a feat performed by God alone, and not by the priest, happening at the time of the Priest's consuming of the Host. The Real Presence influences the Host in a way in which man's ontology restricts his capacity to know, discern, or perceive. Even if the priest were not to consume the Host, it still renders itself available to a material conversion into the Body and Blood by God's witness and power alone and not by man's whatsoever. The priest, instead of crediting himself with knowledge that he cannot possibly possess, can humbly limit himself to the lower ontological estate of knowing and witnessing that he may break bread for the sake of peace, unity, and comfort as it was broken and shared by Abraham and Melchizedek (Genesis 14:18-20).

CHAPTER 6: The Epiclesis & the Threefold Propitiation

The *epiclesis* thus may be comprehended in terms of it being a Eucharistic Epistemology: The Invocation is real because Christ, as Chrysostom repeated, citing Matthew 18:20, is truly present among the body of the Faithful by means of Fellowship; the ordained priest presides over the Sacrament that is eaten, to bring God's Grace through that same Fellowship.

CHAPTER 7: Fellowship & Ecclesiastical Concord Achieved Through the Eucharistic *Anamnesis*

As Aristotle put it, in terms of a person's attainment of civic harmony, it is when citizens enjoy being equipped to participate equally in the *polis* that they can attain *eudaimonia* (happiness in living alongside others). Through cooperation with their fellows, they develop *homonoia* (i.e., concord), developing the friendships that hold communities together and prevent citizens from breaking apart into warring factions (*Politics*; Aristotle; Book II; Sec 1262b:7-9; B.C. 350).

CHAPTER 7: Fellowship & Ecclesiastical Concord Achieved Through the Eucharistic Anamnesis

Even more—but similarly—the Communicants, in following the 1637 and 1928 prayer books' respective Oblations, are imploring Christ to allow us to consume His Body and Blood, and to become One Body with Him:

> And here wee offer and present unto thee, O Lord, our selves, our souls and bodies, to be a reasonable, holy, and lively sacrifice unto Thee, humbly beseeching Thee, that whosoever shall be partakers of this Holy Communion, may worthily receive the most precious Bodie and Bloud of thy Son Jesus Christ, and be fulfilled with thy Grace and heavenly benediction, and made one Bodie with him, that He may dwell in them, and they in Him. (*Book of Common Prayer*; Oblation; 1637)

The Third Propitiation of the Eucharist, would be then, according to Laud:

> ...by every particular man for himself only, and that is the sacrifice of every man's body and soul, to serve Him in both all the rest of his life, for this blessing thus bestowed on him. Now, thus far these dissenting Churches agree, that in the Eucharist there is a sacrifice of duty, and a sacrifice of praise, and a Sacrifice of commemoration of Christ. Therefore, according to the former rule (and here in truth too) it is safest for a man to believe

CHAPTER 7: Fellowship & Ecclesiastical Concord Achieved Through the Eucharistic Anamnesis

> the commemorative, the praising, and the performing Sacrifice, and to offer them duly to God, and leave the Church of Rome in this particular to her superstitions, that I may say no more. (*ibid*, Laud; Sec. 35)

The dedicatory remembrance of the Sacrifice, which is known as the *anamnesis*, is a commemoration of the Passion, and a request that God the Father bless and sanctify the altar gifts occurs throughout the Consecration as the priest holds the Eucharist in his hands:

> Heare us, O mercifull Father, we most humbly beseech thee, and of thy almighty goodnesse vouchsafe so to blesse and sanctifie with thy word and holy Spirit these thy gifts and creatures of bread and wine, that they may bee unto us the Body and Bloud of thy most dearly beloved Son; so that wee receiving them according to thy Sonne our Saviour Jesus Christs holy institution, in remembrance of His death and passion, may be partakers of the same, His most precious Body and Bloud: Who in the night that He was betrayed, took bread, and when He had given thanks, He brake it, and gave it to His disciples, saying, Take, eat, this is my body, which is given for you; do this in remembrance of me. Likewise, after supper He took the cup, and when He had given thanks, he gave it to

them, saying, Drinke yee all of this, for this is my bloud of the new testament, which is shed for you, and for many, for the remission of sins : do this as oft as ye shall drink it in remembrance of me. (*ibid;* Prayer of Consecration; 1637)

By this, the human spirit enters into the Paschal Mystery discernibly, through remembrance of these deeds and words of Jesus. The coming to the table of the Prayer of Humble Access, which Bellarmine could have otherwise imagined—using his "adduction" idea—as being the *calling back* of a person toward the Heart of the Creator, is to associate the beckoning of one's Prevenient Grace toward the prize of Salvation before it empties, by way of *kenosis,* so that God's Grace may preside over the Communicant.

The soul of each Communicant, through the Eucharist, is conjoined in remembrance with the Paschal Mystery as a spiritual recollection of Truth, a benefit of the true *anamnesis* of being known by God and thus associated with Logos (and the Passion of Christ) before one's birth (Jeremiah 1:5).[2] This is able to be achieved by the words of the Liturgy, recognizing the returning toward oneness with the Father, by Whom

---

[2] True Christian *anamnesis* is distinguished from Platonic *anamnesis*—a concept entertained by Plato based on his instruction by Socrates—which refers to the recollection of "innate knowledge" before birth, which Plato claimed (not unlike New Agers today) one can rediscover within oneself.

CHAPTER 7: Fellowship & Ecclesiastical Concord Achieved Through the Eucharistic Anamnesis

Salvation brings the soul into ultimate *theosis* with God.

The Christian view of *anamnesis* is historically a refutation of the error of the pagan theory of Reincarnation, which was firstly proposed by Socrates. He had been asked by his old student, Meno, how a person can discern what is good without firstly having prior knowledge in one's life about it (*Meno*; Plato; Sec. 80:d, 86:b; B.C. 380). The perfect Sacrifice of Christ defines the ultimate goodness as reachable, and thus the *anamnesis* of the Eucharist gives the Christian comprehension of true virtue by the Grace of God that leads him to die to the uses of sin (Romans 6:11) and partake in Communion with the priest and his fellow believers.

In summary, the Eucharistic Liturgy, for Laud, is not merely a blessed rhetorical device but a Holy Anaphora, the extraordinary heart of the Canon of the Mass. It is the Great Thanksgiving, the denouement of the Anglican ordinal that celebrates and shares the Eucharist, during which the elements of bread and wine are consecrated by the priest, are therein characterized by the Real Presence, and are eaten by both priest and communicants, all of whom are given a spiritual glimpse of Eternal Life through this commemorative participation in the Paschal Mystery.

CHAPTER 8: The Intention of the Priest, or Did It Matter Whatsoever Whether William Laud Was a Nice Person?

Pamphlet celebrating Laud's downfall.

CHAPTER 8: *The Intention of the Priest, or Did It Matter Whatsoever Whether William Laud Was a Nice Person?*

In reviewing the professional behavior of Archbishop Laud and his monarchic patron Charles, one wonders how or *if* divine inspiration could have motivated their concern over the infallibility of the Church of England.

William Laud was born in 1573, was named Archbishop of Canterbury in 1633, and was King Charles I's principal ecclesiastical advisor for several years before he became the most prominent of a new generation of churchmen who disliked many of the more Reformist ritual practices that had developed during the reign of Queen Elizabeth I. Although bitterly opposed by the Puritans, the Church of England was in Laud's view in direct continuity with the Medieval Church; Laud, moreover, stressed the unity of Church and State, exalting the role of the king as the Supreme Governor. Charles I was basically being handed the mantle of a Protestant Supreme Pontiff by an able theologian under the aegis of the Divine Right of Kings.[3]

---

[3] "In European history, a political doctrine in defense of monarchical absolutism, which asserted that kings derived their authority from God and could not therefore be held accountable for their actions by any earthly authority such as a parliament. Originating in Europe, the divine-right theory can be traced to the medieval conception of God's award of temporal power to the political ruler, paralleling the award of spiritual power to the church" (*Brittanica*).

CHAPTER 8: The Intention of the Priest, or Did It Matter Whatsoever Whether William Laud Was a Nice Person?

Detail, King Charles I of England. Portrait by Anthony Van Dyck, 1635-6.

Laud emphasized the importance of the priesthood and the sacraments, particularly the Eucharist, and caused consternation among the Reformists by insisting on returning the altar to its pre-Reformation position—that is, against the eastern wall of the nave of the church—and hedging the apse about with Communion rails. He also gave the altar prominent centrality, remanding the pulpit to the left-hand, or Gospel side, of the chancel as viewed by the Congregation from the nave.

A letter containing "additional diocesan instructions" from Laud on altar placement was produced during his trial in the Long Parliament for High Treason. It was written by Laud to his former Commissary of the Diocese of Canterbury, Nathaniel Brent, who had become his hostile enemy (the bracketed areas denote gaps in the letter):

CHAPTER 8: The Intention of the Priest, or Did It Matter Whatsoever Whether William Laud Was a Nice Person?

Salutem in Christo. I am informed that in the parish church of Maidston which is a very populous place the comunion [ ] which cannot butt bee a scandall to many devout and well minded people. These are therfore to require you [ ] upper end of the chancell, and there sett [ ] a decent raile to bee made before and att each side of the same that soe it may be kept from the abuses [ ] if you will distinctly putt in practice in all other places [ ] Gods grace, and rest your loving freind, W: Cant. (*Manuscripts of the House of Lords*, XI [new series]; Historical Manuscripts Commission; The Addenda, 1515-1714 [1962], p. 398; Cited in *The Historical Journal;* Kenneth Fincham; Vol. 44, No. 4; pp. 919-940; London: Dec., 2001)

CHAPTER 8: *The Intention of the Priest, or Did It Matter Whatsoever Whether William Laud Was a Nice Person?*

As head of the Courts of High Commission and the infamous Star Chamber, Laud was abhorred for his harsh sentencing of prominent Puritans and Presbyterians who did not carry out his instructions, or who actively opposed him. Laud identified himself with the unpopular policies of King Charles I and his father James I, and his support for the Bishops' Wars against Scotland in 1639 and 1640, along with his efforts to make the Church independent of Parliament, made him widely disliked. He was ultimately impeached for treason by the Long Parliament in 1640, and finally beheaded on January 10, 1645.

CHAPTER 8: The Intention of the Priest, or Did It Matter Whatsoever Whether William Laud Was a Nice Person?

It would be comforting to hope that Laud had inherited his bad reputation only by proxy. Appointed by the autocratic-absolute King Charles I, who ruled without recourse to Parliament, Archbishop Laud was expected to institute Romish changes without ever holding Synods, just as Charles's Personal Rule implied that Parliament was never to be called into session. This "state within a state" menace, as it was perceived by their opponents, was actually contrary to the position Laud himself established for the priest at the altar, enjoying his incardination in a graceful Diocese, that by Grace he must profess, "*intentionem faciendi quod facit Ecclesia*," that "They, in the common received Doctrine of the Church of Rome, are three: The Matter, the Form, and the Intention of the Prieſt, to do that which the Church doth" (*ibid*, Laud; Sec. 35).

Therefore, because the **Intention of the Priest** is to eat and share the Eucharist, and to act with Grace according to the Bible and the formularies of his Church, the priest's manifest sincerity and overall integrity impacts the Faith of the communicants in their belief in the Sacrament. It would be impossible for the Roman priest to intend that Transubstantiation could reasonably endow the Communicant with Grace if he himself did not at least believe in it. Surely he would need some visible sincerity and appear

CHAPTER 8: *The Intention of the Priest, or Did It Matter Whatsoever Whether William Laud Was a Nice Person?*

earnest even though he cannot attest to having real knowledge that the material conversion of the Host has taken place.

There was also back and forth about Donatism between Laud and Fisher, as to whether a priest's life must be faultless in order for his sacraments to be valid. Faith by the communicants, expressed Laud, was vital for them to believe that Grace was influencing them during Communion without mistrust of the priest that would hamper their capacity to believe. By this token, an evil priest would affect the congregation's capacity to collaborate faithfully with the sacrament. This dilemma calls to mind Laud's sympathy toward Arminianism and that he was hated all the more for it by the Convenanters. Arminians were reviled as Semi-Pelagians in that they famously contended that God's Grace was not "Irresistible." In other words, a bad priest does not help matters at the altar.

Hence if his *anaphora* is merely a craft accomplished by a mistaken minister only doing what the rest of his denomination does and not believing in his work, then Laud, even though widely hated by everyone but the poor—and despite how he mutilated his enemies[4] in the

---

[4] A detailed account of such mutilations can be found toward the end of this chapter.

CHAPTER 8: The Intention of the Priest, or Did It Matter Whatsoever Whether William Laud Was a Nice Person?

Star Chamber, making them his "footstool"—was nevertheless meanwhile exemplifying the correct Matter, Form, and Belief, and thus could been said to have had good Priestly Intention at the Anglican altar. That is, during his tenure at Canterbury it can only be hoped that his sincere belief in his execution of correct Anglican Form allowed the Real Presence to fill his communicants with Grace—but only insofar as their disgust with him did not restrain part of their capacity to participate faithfully in the Sacrament. However, because his illicit behavior in the Star Chamber caused Laud personal adversity and public outrage, the Grace that could have uplifted his Canterbury subjects was surely in part resisted by them.

Two passages—one from Hebrews and the other from Psalms—frame the influence of overall Priestly Intention:

> And every priest standeth daily ministering and offering oftentimes the same sacrifices, which can never take away sins: But this man, after he had offered one sacrifice for sins for ever, sat down on the right hand of God; From henceforth expecting till his enemies be made his footstool. For by one offering he hath perfected for ever them that are sanctified. (Hebrews 10:11-14)

CHAPTER 8: The Intention of the Priest, or Did It Matter Whatsoever Whether William Laud Was a Nice Person?

The above Hebrews passage is based on the following Psalm:

> Sacrifice and offering thou didst not desire; mine ears hast thou opened: burnt offering and sin offering hast thou not required. Then said I, Lo, I come: in the volume of the book it is written of me, I delight to do thy will, O my God: yea, thy law is within my heart. (Psalm 40:6-8; see also Hebrews 10:5-7)

The truth of God's begetting of Christ, the *Body* that was prepared for sacrifice (Hebrews 10:5), had reached the ears of the Psalmist. He adds that our Creator was *not* desirous of Sacrifice of real flesh at the altar more than what Christ did as the Propitiation. Instead, God's interest is in seeing that His Will of peace is done by the minister, indicating that the saintly use of that Priestly Intention, inside and outside of the Sanctuary, fulfills the Father's Will obediently and affects the Congregation always.

God has literally "set apart"(i.e., made holy) the Sacrifice of the Mass, that of remembrance, while intending that the priest obey, during his entire life, not merely the rubrics and formularies of his denomination, executed with sincerity, but the *Father's Will*. Many Old Testament passages, such as Jeremiah 31:31-34, herald the coming of a New Covenant that is

CHAPTER 8: The Intention of the Priest, or Did It Matter Whatsoever Whether William Laud Was a Nice Person?

contingent on obedience by both the priests and all the people. The old sacrifices of animal flesh were intended as but a metaphor for the true Propitiation of sins that was later given to man in Christ, the true Lamb of God: Christ's Body, which He offered up, and Christ's Blood, which was shed, is celebrated on the Christian altar in the *anamnesis* that results in true Propitiation.

Therefore, the Intention of the Priest must not merely be exemplified during the Liturgy but must also both follow the *Form* of obedience and oblige the *Matter* of saintly quotidian during the whole of his life. Laud, who improved Ecclesiology by instituting the 1637 *Book of Common Prayer* and enforcing altar centrality, might be better understood in terms of the contrite, prayerful way in which he submitted himself to be publicly executed (see Chapter 10) than in terms of how he treated his enemies. Despite his issuance of extreme corporal punishments, Anglican Christians should recognize in Laud his Priestly intention to do the Father's Will in defending the Church against abuses. Laud, who accepted his decapitation gracefully, published a profound Eucharistic Liturgy and instituted many useful, permanent improvements to the Anglican Church. He was not merely the cause of "Laudianism" (that is, when that term is used in the pejorative sense).

CHAPTER 8: *The Intention of the Priest, or Did It Matter Whatsoever Whether William Laud Was a Nice Person?*

The reforms of William Laud remain to this day as a testament to his Priestly Intention.

> A good name is better than precious ointment; and the day of death [is more important] than the day of one's birth. (Ecclesiastes 7:1)

In the struggle to understand Laud, it's important to put him in historical context. He operated during the period in English history from 1629 to 1640, when the English monarch believed he had a divine right to unchecked sovereignty (see the definition of the Divine Right of Kings, provided earlier). That royal prerogative was passed along to the Canterbury Chancery, as if via the flow chart of a pontificate acting as a sacerdotal monarch. There appeared to be nothing preventing Laud and Charles from reviving Episcopal and Sarum theology with complementary Tridentine cosmetics within English and Scottish churches, and this led to extreme negative reaction and rebellion. Perhaps not surprisingly for the time period, Laud imposed harsh religious pogroms against his Calvinist Covenanter and Puritan opponents.

CHAPTER 8: *The Intention of the Priest, or Did It Matter Whatsoever Whether William Laud Was a Nice Person?*

Bursting into churches to riot against the instituting of Abp. William Laud's 1637 Book of Common Prayer, *indignant Covenanters, Presbyterians, Puritans, Anabaptists, Levelers, Separatists, Quakers, and others threw the new prayer books, stones, furniture, and various debris at the altars.*

Besides excommunicating them, Laud sent them to prison or had them flogged or pilloried, and in the case of Puritans such as the politician William Prynne, and as regards the anti-Episcopal pamphleteers William Burton and the physician John Bushwick, Laud would have their ears sliced off.

To be fair in comparing the two archbishops of very different eras, the Permanently Interim Archbishop—the ecclesiastical cowboy mentioned in Chapter 1 of this book—never did anything as cruel as Laud did.

CHAPTER 8: The Intention of the Priest, or Did It Matter Whatsoever Whether William Laud Was a Nice Person?

Many of Laud's victims had the initials, "S.L." (for "Seditious Libeler") branded by Laud's ministers upon their foreheads. Because accusations in the Laudian Star Chamber were issued only in Ecclesiastical Latin, Reformists were unable to defend themselves if they could not translate the charges into English. Further humiliating to the Puritans was Laud's reinstitution of public sport competitions on the Sabbath day (Saturday). Boats, on the heels of the Mayflower landing 13 years prior to his appointment to Canterbury, continued sailing for the New World (America).

The Kirk (the Church of Scotland), which had already rejected the attempt by Charles's father, James I, to impose Medieval conventions upon them, was in no mood for Laud's 1637 rewrite of their own *Book of Common Prayer* which had been ratified by the Parliament of Scotland. (Note that Laud's revision contained 12 chapters from Ecclesiasticus and the Book of Wisdom on six saints days, a nod to the Roman Catholic Church). Besides failing to convert the Scottish Presbytery into an Episcopate, James had fared no better in attempting to institute the Five Articles of Perth upon the Kirk. This writ had commanded kneeling during Holy Communion; private Baptism; private Communion for the sick or infirm; Confirmation by a Bishop; and the mandatory celebration of the Holy Days of

CHAPTER 8: *The Intention of the Priest, or Did It Matter Whatsoever Whether William Laud Was a Nice Person?*

Christmas and Easter. The Presbyterian Scotts wanted no part of this and were on guard.

Twelve years later, during a riot over the 1637 revision, the upstart National Covenant of Scotland ordered the bishops to be removed from the Kirk and burned all the new 1637 prayer books, chasubles, and ornaments (the Covenanters were certainly not appeased at Laud's use of the term "Presbyter" in place of "Bishop" in the new book). Out of outraged concern to preserve the Office of Bishops, Charles I myopically declared war upon the Scots, calling the English Parliament twice into session to fund his hostility, and, as the first of the Bishops' Wars led to the Second, Laud and his king grew ever more hated among the Puritans in England and the Calvinists in Scotland—all the more because they curried support among the unpopular Arminians (whose Soteriology held that God's Grace is not irresistible and needs to be obliged by man through his Free Will to choose the path to Salvation).

CHAPTER 8: *The Intention of the Priest, or Did It Matter Whatsoever Whether William Laud Was a Nice Person?*

The Presbyterian Covenanters of Scotland

As Parliament prevailed during two momentous waves of resultant civil wars, conflicts that bled into the Wars of the Three Kingdoms, these two men—Laud and Charles I—were impeached and beheaded in 1645 and 1654, respectively.

The Rump Parliament that was eventually created by the Puritan re-conqueror of Ireland, the militant Oliver Cromwell, ultimately suppressed the bloody, multitiered conflict. After the Et Cetera Oath[5] proved impossible to enforce upon the eventual impeachment by Parliament of 25 of the Bishops, Cromwell, who had co-founded the Root and Branch movement to prosecute and

---

[5] Under Laud, the Long Parliament enacted the "Et Cetera Oath" in 1640, an ordinance within its Canons of that year, decreeing that no one may enact a rule or doctrine that opposes the doctrine, discipline, or government established in the Church of England, or that would attempt to produce standards impelling to its subjection to the See of Rome.

CHAPTER 8: The Intention of the Priest, or Did It Matter Whatsoever Whether William Laud Was a Nice Person?

nullify all aspects of English Episcopacy, was now the "Lord Protector" of England, abolishing ecclesiastical courts and ensuring the destruction of altar rails, surplices, prayer books, and altars. Puritans were in power in England for 11 years.

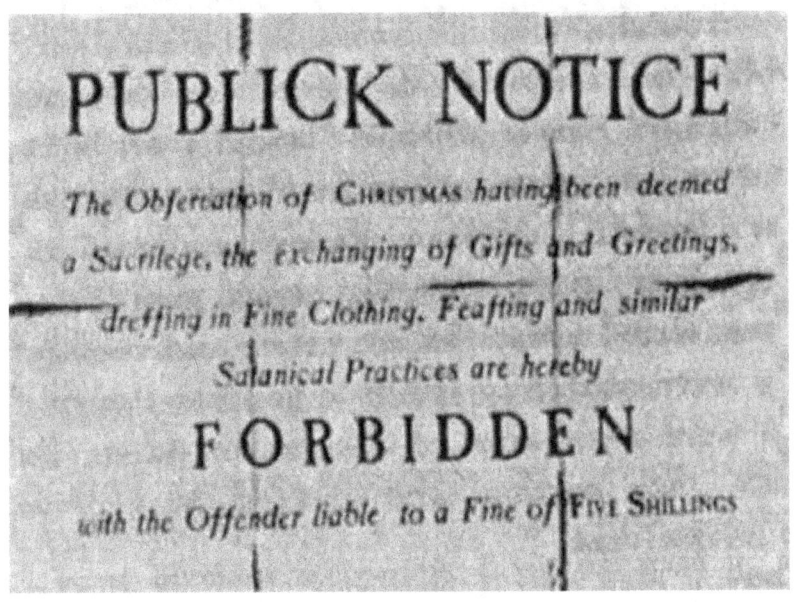

Oliver Cromwell's warning against gift-giving on Christmas.

CHAPTER 8: The Intention of the Priest, or Did It Matter Whatsoever Whether William Laud Was a Nice Person?

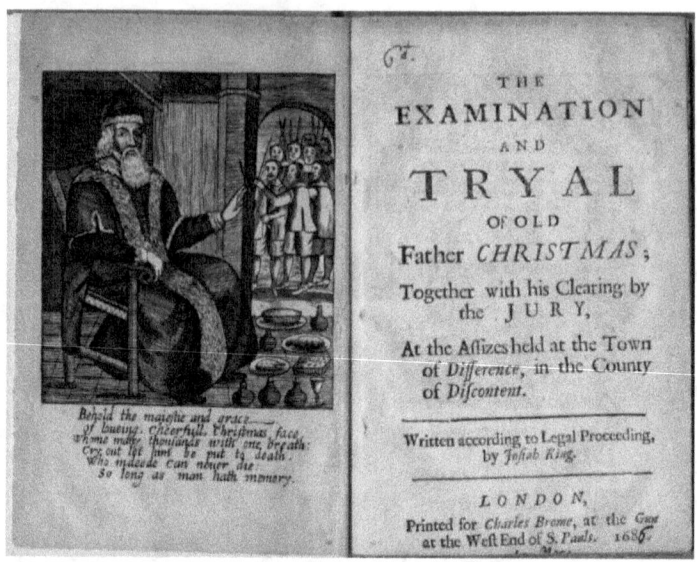

Cromwell puts Santa Claus on Trial, post mortem.

CHAPTER 8: *The Intention of the Priest, or Did It Matter Whatsoever Whether William Laud Was a Nice Person?*

Although the Lord Protector, Cromwell, has outlawed Santa Claus and Christmas gift-giving, along with most forms of entertainment, Englishmen are depicted still welcoming Father Christmas.

The Office of Bishop and most of Laud's Anglo-Catholic changes were eventually revived when this Interregnum finally ended upon Cromwell's death, whereupon the Stuart Monarchy was restored in 1660. The new 1662 revision of the *Book of Common Prayer* found better success throughout the British Isles, remaining mostly untouched in the 1928 version, which is used throughout the Traditional Anglican Church of America (TACA) to this day.

CHAPTER 8: *The Intention of the Priest, or Did It Matter Whatsoever Whether William Laud Was a Nice Person?*

King William III and Mary of Orange, who ushered in the "Glorious Revolution" of 1688, encouraged greater dialogue with dissenters. This is when the "Latitude Men" from Cambridge University, urging a less dogmatic but more inclusive and Broad Church, devised a *via media*, which stemmed from the ideas of Richard Hooker, allowing both High- and Low-Church forms to coexist in England.

So bitterly memorable were the rioting and wars in Britain during those decades that the Act by which Parliament, in 1647, mandated the protection of targeted controversial ministers during religious conflicts (and the apprehension of their antagonists) is still held valid and lawful.

> Imprisonment of Disturbers: Sequestred Ministers interrupting such as are placed in their Livings shall be apprehended.; Imprisonment; Tythes to be paid to them.; Committee for plundered Ministers and for complaints... It is lastly ordered and Ordained, That if any such scandalous or Delinquent Minister put out as aforesaid, their Aiders or Abettors, shall at any time hereafter disturb, molest, or hinder such Minister as is put into such Church or Chappel as aforesaid, in the exercising of the Office of his Ministry, upon proof thereof

CHAPTER 8: *The Intention of the Priest, or Did It Matter Whatsoever Whether William Laud Was a Nice Person?*

>made upon the Oath of two Witnesses, before the said Sheriffs, Majors, Bailiffs, Justices of Peace, Deputy-Lieutenants, or Committees of Parliament, or any two of them; it shall and may be lawfull to and for the said Sheriffs, Majors, Bailiffs, Justices of the Peace, Deputy-Lieutenants, or Committees of Parliament, or any two of them, to commit such Offendor or Offendors to Prison for one Moneth, so often as he or they shall so offend. ("An Ordinance for Keeping in Godly Ministers, Placed in Livings by Authority of Parliament": August 1647; *Acts and Ordinances of the Interregnum, 1642-1660*; C. H. Firth, R.S. Rait, ed.; pp. 999-1,000; London: 1911)

As a result of this law, the *1637 Book of Common Prayer* was not merely preserved from being thrown at clerics but remained in force in England following Laud's and Charles I's executions, all during the years of the Interregnum, and the period of Oliver Cromwell, and throughout the Restoration and the reign of Charles II.

Despite the failed efforts of the Presbyterians, at the 1661 Savoy Conference, to institute the *Alternative Service Book* in Scotland, the tradition of lay verbal participation in Common Prayer was retained for England. For instance, more than their sole saying of "Amen" that had been

CHAPTER 8: The Intention of the Priest, or Did It Matter Whatsoever Whether William Laud Was a Nice Person?

demanded by the Presbyterians, the laity kept its vocal parts during services for the 1662 version; as previously stated, the contents of the 1662 book have been preserved majorly intact throughout the 1928 revision that is used today by Traditional Anglicans.

CHAPTER 9: Bringing Forward Richard Hooker's *Via Media* Eucharistic Theology

A much humbler and more peaceful churchman in comparison to William Laud, Elizabethan theologian Richard Hooker was the Master and Reader of the Temple Church of London, the symbolic head of the Knights Templar who were said to have built it. He had no real jurisdiction besides being appointed to this peculiar chapel by Queen Elizabeth I. He wrote his *Lawes* 88 years prior to the Latitudinarians' discovery of his masterpiece, with its scholarly way of avoiding "The sense that one had special instructions from God [which] made individuals less amenable to moderation and compromise, or to reason itself" (*From Colonials to Provincials,*

CHAPTER 9: Bringing Forward Hooker's Via Media Eucharistic Theology

American Thought and Culture 1680-1760; Ned Landsman; p. 64; Ithaca: Cornell University Press, 1997).

Hooker, whose influence initiated the "Broad Church" movement (for Continuing Anglicanism and Reformed Episcopalism, allowing a continuum from the Low Church of the Reformist example to the High Church of the Tridentine Latin example), understood that something inexplicably mystical happens when the consecrated bread and wine are consumed:

> Christ affirming this heavenly banquet with his personal and true preference doth by His own divine power add to the natural substance thereof supernatural efficacy which additional to the nature of those consecrated elements changeth them and maketh them that unto us which otherwise they could not be; that to us they are thereby made such instruments as mystically, yet truly ineffibly, yet really work our Communion or Fellowship with the person of Jesus Christ as well in that Hee is man as God. (*On the Lawes of Ecclesiastical Politie;* Hooker, Richard; Book V; Chapter 67; 1611)

CHAPTER 9: Bringing Forward Hooker's Via Media Eucharistic Theology

Of greatest importance, says Hooker, is that the Communicant is blessedly changed by the Eucharist, accomplishing the end of peace and the putting away of worry and strife.

> These things I have spoken unto you, that in Me ye might have peace. In the world ye shall have tribulation: but be of good cheer; I have overcome the world. (John 16:33).

The Faithful should abandon, Hooker continues, investigations into Substantiation. In fact, he shifts the focus to how the believer himself is changed. To Hooker, believers are themselves transmuted into loving, peaceful brethren simply by partaking faithfully in the altar Sacrifice:

> Christ assisting this heavenly banquet with his personal and true presence ... by His owne divine power and to the natural substance thereof supernatural efficacie, which in addition to the nature of those consecrated elements changes them and makes them that unto us which otherwise they could not be; that to us they are thereby made such instruments as mystical yet truly, invisible yet really work our communion or fellowship with the person of Jesus Christ as well in that He is man as God, our participation also in the fruit,

CHAPTER 9: Bringing Forward Hooker's Via Media Eucharistic Theology

> Grace, and efficacy of his Body and Blood, that of all the ancient Fathers of the Church any one did ever conceive or imagine other than only a mystical participation of Christ's, both, Body and Blood, in the Sacrament. Neither are their speeches concerning the change of the elements themselves into the Body and Blood of Christ such, that a man can thereby in conscience assure himself it was their meaning to persuade the world either of a corporal Consubstantiation of Christ which those fancified or blessed elements, or of the like Transubstantiation of them into the Body and Blood of Christ. (*ibid*, Hooker; Chapter 67)

CHAPTER 10: Considering That the Contrite Laud Repented Just Before He Was Beheaded

William Laud, sentenced to death for the crime of treason, made the following prayer before paying a gratuity to his executioner for his own beheading:

"Lord, I am coming as fast as I can. I know I must pass through the shadow of death before I can come to see Thee. But it is but umbra mortis, a mere shadow of death, a little darkness upon nature; but thou by Thy merits and passion hast broken through the jaws of death. So, Lord, receive my soul, and have mercy upon me; and bless this kingdom with peace and plenty, and with brotherly love and charity, that there may not be this effusion of Christian blood amongst them for Jesus Christ His sake, if it be Thy will." Then he gave the Lord's Prayer (*A Lecture Delivered Before*

CHAPTER 10: Considering That the Contrite Laud Repented Just Before He Was Beheaded

> *the Students of the General Theological Seminary*; February 6, 1912; Rev. Lucius Waterman D.D.; New York: 1919).

Suddenly, on a trolling expedition, an Irish Puritan by the name of Sir John Clotworthy climbed up the scaffold and belittled the condemned Laud by demanding to hear what "single word" should express the spiritual foundation upon which the doomed Archbishop should expect Christ to receive his prayer, "*Cupio dissolvi et esse cum Christo*" (translated as "I desire to be dissolved and to be with Christ"). The Latin phrase comes from the Vulgate translation of Philippians 1:23-24, in which the Apostle begs:

> *Coartor autem e duobus desiderium habens dissolvi et cum Christo esse multo magis melius / permanere autem in carne magis necessarium est propter vos*" or, "But I am straightened between two: having a **desire to be dissolved and to be with Christ**, a thing by far the better. But to abide still in

CHAPTER 10: Considering That the Contrite Laud Repented Just Before He Was Beheaded

> the flesh, is needful for you" (Philippians 1:21-24).[6]

Certainly Laud was a controversial figure: At stake for English speakers, in his view, was the infallibility of their Church even during the era of its birth pangs. To Laud, restoring ancient tradition should produce a cohesive orthodoxy and unity among the Faithful. But how did his enemies—in Parliament, or among the Presbyterian Scottish Covenanters and Puritan fanatics—perceive this example of a redeemed soul? We return to the taunts and jeers of one Sir John Clotworthy, who demanded that Laud express a "single word" to prove that Christ would hear his prayers:

> Laud's answers to his tormentor were, "No man can express [the assurance]," because "It is to be found within," and "That word is the knowledge of Jesus Christ and that alone" ... Accustomed to seeing order and giving commands, Laud requested that the sight of his decapitation be shielded from the watchful poor, whom he believed adored him, and that the scaffolding

---

[6] In these verses, Saint Paul, during his imprisonment in Rome, is telling the Faithful that he will maintain his Fellowship as it is wanted by the Beloved, even though separation from the body as a prelude to joining Christ is what his soul desires *more*, because "For me to live is Christ and to die is gain."

CHAPTER 10: Considering That the Contrite Laud Repented Just Before He Was Beheaded

should be cleared of other condemned men and their parties so that he would have room to die. It was as if he were setting a table the way he wanted. (*ibid*, Waterman)

It should be noted that during Laud's "trial" in 1644, the letter of instructions to Brent, written during the 1630s, was accepted to support the Ordinance of Attainder,[7] a writ that is used by a legislature in the absence of proof that the accused has committed treason.

---

[7] The United States Constitution forbids legislative bills of attainder: in federal law under Article I, Section 9, Clause 3 ("No Bill of Attainder or *ex post facto* Law shall be passed"), and in state law under Article I, Section 10.

CHAPTER 11: Using Irenaean Theodicy to Contemplate Whether Laud's Suffering on the Scaffold Was Sanctifying

St. Irenaeus, Bishop of Lyon and martyr.

Perhaps it would have appeared to his enemies rather hypocritical for Laud, flogger and severer of ears, to have asked God to cease the violence between Christians. However, if it is true that God maintains a certain distance from all people in order that the "knock" of their Free Will may open the door of God's Grace (Matthew 7:7), the so-called Irenaeus Theodicy would be at play here.

Considering that he had four years of imprisonment and thus plenty of time to

CHAPTER 11: Using Irenaean Theodicy to Contemplate Whether Laud's Suffering on the Scaffold Was Sanctifying

contemplate his eventual execution, it should not seem inexplicable that Laud would now utter such a sincere, hopeful prayer on the scaffold. As Irenaeus said, "there is no coercion with God, but a good will [towards us] is present with Him continually." Laud's trials surely must have helped his spirit incorporate the changes that God had cultivated inside him during the Substantive process while he consumed the Eucharist as both priest and archbishop. The purpose of the evils for which he was now welcoming his corporal punishment was the seeding of fertile ground for the growing of Grace within him (2 Peter 3:18), inasmuch as Irenaeus had described the moral improvement that had occurred in Jonah while inside the body of the fish, inspiring Jonah to opt for sincerely preaching at Ninevah (*Adversus Haereses*; Saint Irenaeus of Lyon; Book III, Chapter 20; Book IV; Chapter 37; A.D. 180).

In contrast to Laud, and even 80 years earlier, Hooker always aimed his language at believers like himself, who had already long arrived at the shores of Ninevah at the time of his writing. Chapter 67 of Book V of Hooker's *Lawes* was not particularly aimed at the Puritans, but at all those who deny the Real Presence. As such, it seeks to explain how the Eucharist continues the new life in Christ that begins at Baptism, though always threatened by sin (*ibid*, Hooker; Sec. 1).

CHAPTER 11: Using Irenaean Theodicy to Contemplate Whether Laud's Suffering on the Scaffold Was Sanctifying

The consumed elements were, to Hooker, always mystical and true instruments without question, that "work our communion [*koinonia*] with the person of Jesus Christ," the fruit endowed with that Grace "whereupon there ensues a kind of Transubstantiation in us" (*ibid*, Sec. 11), as mentioned earlier.

By way of Hooker, the *via media* was already begging for fruitless contention to end among English speakers, so that enjoyment of the fruition of the Sacrament could usher forth new Life in the Communicant when it is consumed by God's invisible workings, as all agree that He is truly present (*ibid*, Sec. 7).

CHAPTER 12: Fifty-One Years After Laud's Execution, Hooker's Real-Presence Theology Speaks Across Latitudes

Advocating conciliation between opponents, Hooker's argumentation concentrates on what all the polemicists have in common, agreed though they are in rejecting a singularly commemorative doctrine, in which the sacrament is "a shadow, destitute, empty, and void of Christ" (*ibid*, Sec. 6).

The Reformers, be they Anglican, Zwinglian, Lutheran, or Catholic, affirm a "real participation in Christ and in the life of his Body and Blood by means of this Sacrament" (*ibid*, Sec. 6).
Therefore, why "should the world continue to be

CHAPTER 12: Fifty-One Years After Laud's Execution, Hooker's Real-Presence Theology Speaks Across Latitudes

distracted and torn apart by so many fights, when the only remaining controversy is where Christ is?" (*ibid,* Sec. 6).

Indeed, all parties agree that "the soul of man is the receptacle of Christ's presence" (*ibid,* Sec. 2), so that the disagreement only concerns whether the presence is only there (as the Reformed say) or also somehow in the bread and wine (as the Lutherans and Catholics say in their own distinctive ways).

Hooker laments this as a foolish debate:

> I should wish that men would spend more time meditating with silence on what we have by the sacrament, and less on disputing about how ... Curious and intricate speculations hinder, abate, and quench those inflamed motions of delight and joy which divine graces raise when extraordinarily present to us. (*ibid,* Sec. 6)

Hooker's adoration of the Eucharist, much of it inspired by the book *De Coena Domini* by Arnold De Bonneval (d. 1156), is printed here in its entirety:

> He which has said of the one Sacrament, "wash and be clean," has said concerning the other likewise, "eat and live." If therefore without any such particular and solemn warrant as this is that poor

*CHAPTER 12: Fifty-One Years After Laud's Execution,
Hooker's Real-Presence Theology Speaks Across Latitudes*

distressed woman coming unto Christ for health could so constantly resolve herself, "may I but touch the skirt of his garment I shall be whole," what moves us to argue of the manner how life should come by bread, our duty being here but to take what is offered, and most assuredly to rest persuaded of this, that can we but eat [and have Faith that] we are safe? When I behold with mine eyes some small and scarce discernible grain or seed whereof nature makes promise that a tree shall come, and when afterwards of that tree any skillful artificer undertakes to frame some exquisite and curious work, I look for the event, I move no question about performance either of the one or of the other. Shall I simply credit nature in things natural; shall I in things artificial rely myself on art, never offering to make doubt; and, in that which is above both art and nature refuse to believe the author of both, except he acquaint me with his ways, and lay the secret of his skill before me? Where God himself doth speak those things which either for height and sublimity of matter, or else for secrecy of performance we are not able to reach unto, as we may be ignorant without danger, so it can be no disgrace to confess we are ignorant. Such

CHAPTER 12: Fifty-One Years After Laud's Execution, Hooker's Real-Presence Theology Speaks Across Latitudes

as love piety will as much as in them lieth know all things that God commands, but especially the duties of service which they owe to God. As for his dark and hidden works, they prefer as becometh them in such cases simplicity of faith before that knowledge, which curiously sifting what it should adore, and disputing too boldly of that which the wit of man cannot search, chills for the most part all warmth of zeal, and bringeth soundness of belief many times into great hazard. Let it therefore be sufficient for me presenting myself at the Lord's table to know what there I receive from Him, without searching or inquiring of the manner how Christ performs His promise; let disputes and questions, enemies to piety, abatements of true devotion, and hitherto in this cause but over patiently heard, let them take their rest; let curious and sharpwitted men beat their heads about what questions themselves will, the very letter of the word of Christ giveth plain security that these mysteries do as nails fasten us to His very Cross, that by them we draw out, as touching efficacy, force, and virtue, even the blood of His gored side, in the wounds of our Redeemer we there dip our tongues, we are dyed red both within and without,

CHAPTER 12: Fifty-One Years After Laud's Execution, Hooker's Real-Presence Theology Speaks Across Latitudes

> our hunger is satisfied and our thirst for ever quenched; they are things wonderful which he feels, great which he sees and unheard of which he utters, whose soul is possessed of this Paschal Lamb and made joyful in the strength of this new wine. This bread hath in it more than the substance which our eyes behold, this cup hallowed with solemn benediction avails to the endless life and welfare both of soul and body, in that it serves as well for a medicine to heal our infirmities and purge our sins as for a sacrifice of thanksgiving; what these elements are in themselves it skills not; it is enough that to me which take them [that] they are the Body and Blood of Christ, His promise in witness hereof suffices, his word he knows which way to accomplish; why should any cogitation possess the mind of a faithful communicant but this, "O my God thou art true, O my Soul thou art happy." (*ibid*, Sec. 11)

An Episcopate and its congregants may rest assured that the Grace freely given through Faith by God is sufficient for their Salvation (Ephesians 2:8-9). Who else is needed to rule Christendom except resultantly jubilant, upright Bishops and Presbyters who are thus blameless,

CHAPTER 12: Fifty-One Years After Laud's Execution, Hooker's Real-Presence Theology Speaks Across Latitudes

sober, vigilant, and who exhibit honesty and self-control (1 Timothy 3:2-12)?

> But avoid foolish questions, and genealogies, and contentions, and strivings about the law; for they are unprofitable and vain. (Titus 3:9)

The next chapter concerns remarkable terms concerning the sacraments—terms seldom taught in today's institutional churches but ones worthy to be learned anew during Catechesis. The presentation of these terms is intended so that sober and blameless concord will result from an enhanced understanding of how God involves Himself in traditional church life.

CHAPTER 13: How the Sacramental Christian Participates in the Fullness of the Triune Godhead

Perichoresis *is the interpenetration of each of the three persons of the Triune Godhead. During the Mass, the churchgoer "gazes upon" the beauty of profound Truth in God and the Liturgy and thus experiences* Theoria. At *Holy Communion,* Perichoresis *connects everyone involved, and later at Salvation,* Theosis *is the joining of the saved person in Oneness with the Godhead.*

The sharing of Holy Communion between the communicants and the Priest, all of whom eat and drink the Body and Blood, enjoins these partakers with the fullness of the Holy Trinity.

As we have seen above, Laud and Hooker explained the supernatural role of the communicant and Priest throughout the *anaphora*.

CHAPTER 13: How the Sacramental Christian Participates in the Fullness of the Triune Godhead

But, within this supernatural Fellowship, the three-way interpenetration of the Father, the Son, and the Holy Spirit, incorporates this fourth mortal collaborator—the priest and communicants—to complete a unified Form with the Triune Godhead, which gives rise to *theosis* upon Salvation for each person. *Theosis* and several other terms will be defined within this chapter.

Although it is an idea defined in the early Church, the idea of *interpenetration* within the Holy Trinity, known as *perichoresis* (defined, below), along with other related theological concepts, is not a subject that most congregations give attention to today.

However, Traditional Anglicanism remains grounded in the teaching of orthodox texts that are based on the Bible. If it did not, then it would be at risk for employing heterodoxy and heresy that would expose unwitting Christians to the profane and sordid uses of false teachers, who would "make merchandise" out of them (2 Peter 2:3). The goal of this writing is not to follow the wide road of so many churches in these End Times.

> For my mouth shall speak Truth; and wickedness is an abomination to my lips. (Proverbs 8:7)

CHAPTER 13: How the Sacramental Christian Participates in the Fullness of the Triune Godhead

In other words, although institutional churches may intend otherwise, the Liturgy and Sacraments must be taught according to the Canon of a church, which bases its catechesis upon the Bible and the writings of the Apostolic and Church Fathers. The formularies of an *ecclesia*, which seeks God's blessings for its good work of explicating Logos, will make a Congregation become one of the churches like Smyrna and Philadelphia (Revelation 1: 11). Otherwise, its ministries will be in error.

> Therefore to Him that knoweth to do good, and doeth it not, to him it is sin. (James 4:17)

Thus, important terms like *perichoresis*, among others, will be defined below, primarily through texts taken from several of the ancient fathers.

Homoousios: That God the Son and God the Father are of one (i.e., the same) substance. This is the definitive doctrine about Jesus being God decided at the Council of Nicaea (A.D. 325), the first ecumenical council whereby this orthodox understanding of Christology formulated the Nicene Creed.

Hypostatic Union: The simultaneous humanity and divinity of Christ, who has two natures existing as one person. That is, Christ is both fully man and fully God, a concept defined as the union of *hypostasis* in the Council of

CHAPTER 13: How the Sacramental Christian Participates in the Fullness of the Triune Godhead

Chalcedon (A.D. 450). Synonymous as the "Dyophysite" Christology, the two natures are inseparable as one person.

Perichoresis: The reciprocal existence and interpenetration or coinherence that is shared by the Father, the Son, and the Holy Spirit, which composes the Trinity/Triune Godhead. In Greek the term is Περιχώρηση or *perichorei*, and in English it is *circumincession* (defined as "going around" [circum-] and "marching or stepping along together in Eternity" [-incession]).

This mystical relationship begins to share itself with a Christian during the biblical Sacrament of Holy Baptism, when the Holy Spirit can first be said to "indwell" a person. This unity between God and man is fully consummated at the time of one's ultimate Salvation, wherein the Christian becomes one within the Triune Godhead (see *theosis*, below).

Holy Baptism: The biblical Sacrament whereby receipt by the baptized of the indwelling of the Holy Spirit is achieved through his or her Christening by a priest with water in the name of the Father, and of the Son, and of the Holy Spirit. By Holy Baptism, the Christian enters into the Church and becomes part of the Body of Christ. The idea of "Oneness with God" through Baptism, awarded in part at so early a time of one's Christian life (as it usually takes place in

CHAPTER 13: How the Sacramental Christian Participates in the Fullness of the Triune Godhead

one's infancy), also signifies both the Oneness that takes place during Holy Communion and that ultimate Oneness experienced at the time of one's ultimate Salvation[8]:

> For by one Spirit are we all baptized into one body, whether we be Jews or Gentiles, whether we be bond or free; and have been all made to drink into one Spirit. (1 Corinthians 12:13)

The good Christian life of the churchgoer is thereafter pursued by the *putting on* of Christ, the lifelong wearing of the wedding garment (Matthew 22:11).

> For as many of you as have been baptized into Christ have put on Christ. (Galatians 3:27)

---

[8] For it's not only that we *were* saved (Romans 8:24, Ephesians 2:5-8) and that we *are being* saved (1 Corinthians 1:8, 2 Corinthians 2:15) but also that we *will be* saved (Romans 5:9-10, 1 Corinthians 3:12-15).

CHAPTER 13: How the Sacramental Christian Participates in the Fullness of the Triune Godhead

On Sundays, at Holy Communion, this indwelling is shared between the priest and the congregation through their consuming of the Body and Blood of the Lamb during the Eucharistic Liturgy. The resultant unity is the Reciprocal Indwelling (defined below) between the three persons of the Trinity and the Church. Comprehension of this investiture stems from the ancient sources detailed below, beginning with the Word of God, via the process of *theoria* (also defined below).

"I am crucified with Christ: nevertheless I live; yet not I, but Christ liveth in me: and the life which I now live in the flesh I live by the faith of the Son of God, Who loved me, and gave himself for me" (Galatians 2:20). Image, credit, I'll Be David & I'll Be Jonathan, Inc.

CHAPTER 13: How the Sacramental Christian Participates in the Fullness of the Triune Godhead

Therefore, the Holy Sacraments are fulfilled with participation by God, the priest, and the communicants in a state of *perichoresis*. By this mystical system, the Holy Trinity indwells in the person during his Baptism (with Water) and during the partaking of Communion (receiving the Body and Blood of Christ).

The next entry provides a shorthand definition of the supernatural character of the second of the two Sacraments established directly by Christ.

Holy Communion: The sharing and exchanging of profound spiritual Love with God during the Mass, at which the bread and wine are consecrated and shared as the Body and Blood of Christ, where the Triune Godhead, by its *perichoresis*, invests Itself both corporeally and spiritually with baptized believers.

Reciprocal Indwelling: The indwelling of God within us and us within God:

> Herein is love, not that we loved God, but that he loved us, and sent his Son to be the propitiation for our sins. Beloved, if God so loved us, we ought also to love one another. No man hath seen God at any time. If we love one another, God dwelleth in us, and his love is perfected in us. Hereby know we that we dwell in him, and

CHAPTER 13: How the Sacramental Christian Participates in the Fullness of the Triune Godhead

> he in us, because he hath given us of his Spirit. And we have seen and do testify that the Father sent the Son to be the Saviour of the world. Whosoever shall confess that Jesus is the Son of God, God dwelleth in him, and he in God. (1 John 4:10-15)

To cultivate the human mind and spirit for this Communion, the Liturgy of the Word and the Liturgy of the Eucharist are given at Mass and during the saying of the Daily Office.

Theoria: A mystical learning undertaken through the Liturgy of both the Word and Eucharist to comprehend how God acts during the Mass. Known as the *contemplatio* in Latin, and in Greek the θεωρία or *theoria*, it signifies the soulful gazing or looking upon the divinity behind every Sacrament. The Liturgy prepares the soul for the ultimate Oneness with God at Salvation (defined as *theosis*, below).

Augustine of Hippo analyzed the importance of the Liturgy presided over by the priests or elders, as the first means of how God indwells the Faithful.

> The sound of our words strikes the ears, the Master is within... The sound of our words strikes the ears, the Master is within... This then we say to you: whether

CHAPTER 13: How the Sacramental Christian Participates in the Fullness of the Triune Godhead

> we plant, or whether we water, by speaking we are not any thing; but He that giveth the increase, even God: that is, "His unction which teacheth you concerning all things. *(Ten Homilies on the Epistle of John to the Parthians; Saint* Augustine of Hippo; Homily III: 1 John 2:18-27; A.D. 408-421; A.D. 407)

The establishment of the Church throughout the world required the Apostolic Evangelization epitomized by the selfless missionary work performed by Saint Paul of Tarsus, who wrote mightily of this indwelling of God in man through the Oneness we can enjoy through the Holy Sacraments of the Church:

> That He would grant you, according to the riches of His glory, to be strengthened with might by His Spirit in the inner man; That Christ may dwell in your hearts by Faith; that ye, being rooted and grounded in love, may be able to comprehend with all saints what is the breadth, and length, and depth, and height; and to know the love of Christ, which passeth knowledge, that **ye might be filled with all the fulness of God.** (Ephesians 3:16-17).

As Jesus indwells in the person, the *Metaphysics of the Eucharist* may hence be taken to heart together with the soulful brainwork of *theoria* as

CHAPTER 13: How the Sacramental Christian Participates in the Fullness of the Triune Godhead

the *perichoresis* that flows between the priest, communicants, the Father, the Son, and the Holy Spirit.

This Reciprocal Indwelling was taught by the Desert Father, Saint Gregory of Nazianzus, who introduced the idea that the process of human divinization or *theosis* commences during one's life through the indwelling of the Holy Spirit that occurs at Baptism and Holy Communion.

Nazianzus taught that Christ is the Second Man (with Adam being the first, whose personal Ontology did not yet benefit from these Metaphysics):

> For the words, The Second Man is the Lord from Heaven (1 Corinthians 15:47); and, As is the Heavenly, such are they that are Heavenly; and, No man hath ascended up into Heaven save He which came down from Heaven, even the Son of Man which is in Heaven (John 3:13); and the like, are to be understood as said on account of the Union with the heavenly; just as that All Things were made by Christ, (John 1:3) and that Christ dwelleth in your hearts (Ephesians 3:17) is said, not of the visible nature which belongs to God, but of what is perceived by the mind, the names being mingled like the natures, and flowing into one another, according to the law of their

intimate union. (*To Cledonius the Priest against Apollinarius;* Saint Gregory of Nazianzus; Epistle CI; Sec. 5; d. A.D. 390)

The promise of the peace and concord of Heaven, felt extraordinarily by the Faithful through its Fellowship with the Holy Trinity during Holy Communion, signifies that the oneness with the Triune God will be felt in its fullness upon Salvation, as the soul transcends away from the sinful sorrows of life toward eternal life with God. Thus, continues Nazianzus:

> Life and death, as they are called, apparently so different, are in a sense resolved into (*perichorei*; περιχορεσεις), and successive to, each other ... What grievance can we find in being transferred hence to the true life? In being freed from the vicissitudes, the agitation, the disgust, and all the vile tribute we must pay to this life, to find ourselves, amid stable things, which know no flux, while as lesser lights, we circle round the great light [Genesis 1:16]? (*Oration 18;* Gregory of Nazianzus; Sec. 42; d. A.D. 390)

> That in the ages to come He might shew the exceeding riches of His Grace in His kindness toward us through Christ Jesus. (Ephesians 2:7)

CHAPTER 13: *How the Sacramental Christian Participates in the Fullness of the Triune Godhead*

Theosis: Also known as divinization, the phenomenon of a Christian "being made God" (sometimes translated into English as "becoming God"),[9] achieved through Faith (i.e., a childlike Faith in Christ and the promises of God; orthodox belief in and submission to the Word of God); dying to the self (defined, below), or living in a state of humility toward God and man; and receiving the Holy Sacraments of Baptism and Communion. Various verses in the Bible purport that by answering the calling to virtue and glory, the divinization of the person is granted upon Salvation (Psalms 82:6; 2 Corinthians 3:17-18; John 10;33-36). Understood through *theoria*, advancing toward this Oneness signifies Logos, as:

> ... the Word of God, our Lord Jesus Christ, Who did, through His transcendent Love, become what we are, that He might bring us to be even what He is Himself. (*Adversus Haereses*; Saint Irenaeus of Lyon; Book V; Preface; A.D. 180)

---

[9] Although this teaching may sound foreign to the modern Christian ear, recall that Jesus spoke these words, saying, "Is it not written in your law, I said, Ye are gods?" (John 10:34); see also Psalm 82:6-7.

CHAPTER 13: How the Sacramental Christian Participates in the Fullness of the Triune Godhead

> For He was made man that we might be made God[10]; and He manifested Himself by a body that we might receive the idea of the unseen Father; and He endured the insolence of men that we might inherit immortality. (*On the Incarnation of the Word*, Saint Athanasius, 54(3).

Striving toward the state of Grace by dying to the uses of sin maintains the soul in its journey toward this Oneness.

> And be not conformed to this world: but be ye transformed by the renewing of your mind, that ye may prove what is that good, and acceptable, and perfect, will of God. (Romans 12:2)

Dying to the Self: Resisting sin and participating in the Confession and the Forgiveness and Remission of Sin during the Ordinal of Holy Communion renders a person useless for the strategies of the devil and sinful error, so that *theosis* may continue from Baptism, through death, to Salvation and the ultimate Onenesss of the completed *theosis* with the Triune Godhead.

---

[10] Note the Greek verb θεοποιηθῶμεν can alternately be translated as "be made God Himself" or "be made gods."

CHAPTER 13: *How the Sacramental Christian Participates in the Fullness of the Triune Godhead*

> Whereby are given unto us exceeding great and precious promises: that by these ye might be partakers of the divine nature, having escaped the corruption that is in the world through lust. (2 Peter 1:4)

> Likewise reckon ye also yourselves to be dead indeed unto sin, but alive unto God through Jesus Christ our Lord. (Romans 6:11)

Living a humble, selfless Christian life avails the communicant of the Grace associated with the Sacraments in the advance toward full *theosis*:

> [People] were made like God, free from suffering and death, provided that they kept His commandments, and were deemed deserving of the name of His sons, and yet they, becoming like Adam and Eve, work out death for themselves; let the interpretation of the Psalm be held just as you wish, yet thereby it is demonstrated that all men are deemed worthy of becoming "gods," and of having power to become sons of the Highest. (*Dialogue with Trypho;* Saint Justin Martyr; Chapter CXXIV; A.D. 160)

The Christian—avoiding, renouncing, and confessing his sins—who participates in the Word of God and Holy Communion at Mass will enjoy full participation with the Oneness with

CHAPTER 13: How the Sacramental Christian Participates in the Fullness of the Triune Godhead

the Triune God upon his or her Salvation, when *theosis* is fully achieved:

> [The Christian] who listens to the Lord, and follows the prophecy given by Him, will be formed perfectly in the likeness of the teacher—made a god going about in flesh. (*The Stromata, or Miscellanies;* Saint Clement of Alexandria; Book VII; Chapter XVI; A.D. 215).

Traditional Anglicanism distinguishes itself from merely being "Continuing Anglicanism" because it emulates the holy words of the Church Fathers so that the Communion of Saints will benefit from following a virtuous Christian life with enhanced spiritual intelligence, being made aware of the priceless teachings that all Christians have inherited as their birthright, but that by and large they have forgotten.

The following additional passages further explain some of the above concepts, spoken with unparalleled loving concern paid forward for the Salvation of Christians who would live many centuries after the writers died.

Saint Maximus the Confessor, Concerning *Theosis*:

> Deification, briefly, is the encompassing and fulfillment of all times and ages, and of all that exists in either. This encompassing and

CHAPTER 13: How the Sacramental Christian Participates in the Fullness of the Triune Godhead

fulfillment is the union, in the person granted salvation, of his real authentic origin with his real authentic consummation. This union presupposes a transcending of all that by nature is essentially limited by an origin and a consummation. Such transcendence is effected by the almighty and more than powerful energy of God, acting in a direct and infinite manner in the person found worthy of this transcendence. The action of this divine energy bestows a more than ineffable pleasure and joy on him in whom the unutterable and unfathomable union with the divine is accomplished. This, in the nature of things, cannot be perceived, conceived or expressed. *(The Philokalia;* Saint Maximus the Confessor; Vol. 2; Sec. 240)

A sure warrant for looking forward with hope to deification of human nature is provided by the Incarnation of God, which makes man God to the same degree as God Himself became man. ... Let us become the image of the one whole God, bearing nothing earthly in ourselves, so that we may consort with God and become gods, receiving from God our existence as gods. For it is clear that He Who became man without sin (cf. Heb. 4:15) will divinize human nature without changing it into the Divine Nature, and will raise it up for His Own sake to the same degree as He

CHAPTER 13: *How the Sacramental Christian Participates in the Fullness of the Triune Godhead*

> lowered Himself for man's sake. This is what St[.] Paul teaches mystically when he says, "that in the ages to come he might display the overflowing richness of His grace [Ephesians 2:7] (*ibid*, Maximus).

Perichoresis, Explained by Saint John of Damascus:

> Uncreate, without beginning, immortal, infinite, eternal, immaterial , good, creative, just, enlightening, immutable, passionless, uncircumscribed, immeasurable, unlimited, undefined, unseen, unthinkable, wanting in nothing, being His own rule and authority, all-ruling, life-giving, omnipotent, of infinite power, containing and maintaining the universe and making provision for all: all these and such like attributes the Deity possesses by nature, not having received them from elsewhere, but Himself imparting all good to His own creations according to the capacity of each.

> The subsistences dwell and are established firmly in one another. For they are inseparable and cannot part from one another, but keep to their separate courses within one another, without coalescing or mingling, but cleaving to each other. For the Son is in the Father and the Spirit: and

CHAPTER 13: How the Sacramental Christian Participates in the Fullness of the Triune Godhead

the Spirit in the Father and the Son: and the Father in the Son and the Spirit, but there is no coalescence or commingling or confusion. And there is one and the same motion: for there is one impulse and one motion of the three subsistences, which is not to be observed in any created nature.

Further the divine effulgence and energy, being one and simple and indivisible, assuming many varied forms in its goodness among what is divisible and allotting to each the component parts of its own nature, still remains simple and is multiplied without division among the divided, and gathers and converts the divided into its own simplicity. For all things long after it and have their existence in it. It gives also to all things being according to their several natures , and it is itself the being of existing things, the life of living things, the reason of rational beings, the thought of thinking beings. But it is itself above mind and reason and life and essence.

Further the divine nature has the property of penetrating all things without mixing with them and of being itself impenetrable by anything else. Moreover, there is the property of knowing all things with a simple knowledge and of seeing all things, simply with His divine, all-surveying, immaterial eye, both the things of the present, and the things of the past, and the things of the future, before they come into being (Daniel 2:22). It is also sinless, and can cast sin out, and bring salvation: and all that it wills, it can accomplish, but does not will all it could accomplish. For it could destroy the universe but it does not will so to do. (*An Exposition of the Orthodox Faith;* Saint John of Damascus; Book I; Chapter 14: "The properties of the divine nature"; d. A.D. 749).

Orthodox Contemplative Prayer Enhancing Theoria During the Anaphora

There is a concern within much of Christendom that Contemplative Prayer connotes Modernist abuses of the meditative state, implying certain heterodox practices that many institutional Christian denominations have indeed sadly onboarded. Such contemplative Christian societies have adopted pseudoscience, New Thought and New Age ideas, the Kabbalah, the Occult, Centering Prayer, and especially in the latter case, aspects of non-Christian religions and religious practices, such as Buddhism, Devic Mysticism, Muslim Mysticism, Yoga, and Yoruba spirituality.

CHAPTER 13: How the Sacramental Christian Participates in the Fullness of the Triune Godhead

To be sure, weird "Christian" syncretic practices incorporating the Enneagram, Yoga, Ein Sof, Psychoanalysis, Neo-Platonism and Gnosticism, Satanism, Laws of Attraction, or even Quantum Psychology have each been known to cite verses from Scripture to bolster claims that its avenue of meditation deserves to tempt the Christian away from Christ.

However, the truly Christian practice of Contemplative Prayer, which this section of Chapter 13 will cover, springs from ancient writings that are licit, valid, moral, and sound. They each offer doctrinal possibilities for canonical prayer life that not only stay within traditional Anglican formularies but can also deepen spiritual understanding of the Liturgy.

The topic of *theoria* poses the concept of "gnosis" (the Greek word for knowledge) as it was known to Origen, Evagrius Ponticus, and Saint Clement of Alexandria. (It is **not** to be confused with the "gnosis" of the "Gnostic," who does not believe Jesus is the Son of God and who worships the Universe or Satan.) Because gnosis concerns the buttressing of human awareness with mystical knowledge, it is curious that the books of the Apocrypha—books more dedicated to shrewd speculation concerning *noētikos*, defined as the "esoteric Sophia" or "inner wisdom" (Εσωτερική σοφία) than to Faith (namely,

CHAPTER 13: How the Sacramental Christian Participates in the Fullness of the Triune Godhead

the Wisdom of Solomon, Sirach, and Baruch)—were omitted from the King James canon.

Their mode of inspiration owes itself more to a proclivity for esoteric engrossment that was familiar to the Stoic, Platonic, and Neopythagorean pagans Hermes Trismegistus, Pythagoras, Plotinus, Iamblichus, and Philo of Alexandria and thus today motivates Gnostic contemplation rather than the ignition of Hope for the Revelation of the truly begotten Christ.

However, the true spiritual strain of "gnosis" known as *theoria* should be understood within the context of how the Word of God did truly exist before the world was made. "In the beginning was the Word, and the Word was with God, and the Word was God ... All things were made by Him, and without Him was not any thing made that was made" (John 1: 1,3). Furthermore, "all things were created by Him, and for Him: and He is before all things, and by Him all things consist" (Colossians 1:17). And finally, since we know that the Word is Christ and the Word is God, and also that "God is love" (1 John 4:8), we can know with all certainty that Christ is Love.

Wisdom, personified in so many texts (see, e.g., Proverbs 8:22-31; 3:19; Wisdom 8:4-6; Sirach 1:4, 9), was God's *adjunct* in the Creation of all things, not the Creator. The search for Wisdom—

CHAPTER 13: How the Sacramental Christian Participates in the Fullness of the Triune Godhead

even though she is better than most precious things such as rubies (Proverbs 8:11-36)—must always lead in the end to the discovery of Love Himself, Who is God (1 John 4:16):

> But the wisdom that is from above is first pure, then peaceable, gentle, and easy to be intreated, full of mercy and good fruits, without partiality, and without hypocrisy (James 3:17).

Mystical knowledge seeking wisdom, guided only by itself and whose end is only itself—"ever learning and never able to come to the knowledge of the truth" (2 Timothy 3:7)—can lead only to sin, and must be resisted. It is only Faith in Christ that can guide one to everlasting life: "Faith should not stand in the wisdom of men, but in the power of God" (1 Corinthians 2:5).

> For the Jews require a sign, and the Greeks seeketh after wisdom; but we preach Christ crucified, unto the Jews a stumbling block, and unto the Greeks foolishness; but unto them which are called, both Jews and Greeks, Christ the power of God, and the wisdom of God. (1 Corinthians 1:22-24)

CHAPTER 13: How the Sacramental Christian Participates in the Fullness of the Triune Godhead

The options for incrementing spiritual comprehension of the *anaphora* fall far outside of the shadowy influence of contemporary politics and culture only when they come from the ancient orthodox and catholic Church. Otherwise, Christians must:

> Beware lest any man spoil you through philosophy and vain deceit, after the tradition of men, after the rudiments of the world, and not after Christ. (Colossians 2:8)

Theoria therefore must be safely felt as a sharing between Christians and the Holy Trinity of the

CHAPTER 13: How the Sacramental Christian Participates in the Fullness of the Triune Godhead

essence of the omnibenevolent God, so that Salvation for each person signifies their ultimate *theosis*. All who suffer with Christ will be glorified together (Romans 8:17). According to Saint John Climacus, Love is therefore:

> "... the linking together of the supreme trinity among the virtues" which he said is threefold, "Agape, Hope, and Faith [Περὶ ἀγάπης, ἐλπίδος καὶ πίστεως]." (*The Ladder of Divine Ascent*; Saint John Climacus; Trans. Archimandrite Lazarus Moore; Step 30; Intro.; A.D. 600)

Climacus continued:

> The first [Love] can make and create all things; the divine mercy surrounds the second [Hope] and makes it immune to disappointment; the third [Faith] does not fall, does not stop in its course and allows no respite to him who is wounded by its blessed rapture. (*ibid*, Climacus; Step 30; Sec. 3)

Standing at the ultimate height of wisdom:

> Love bestows prophecy; love yields miracles; love is an abyss of illumination; love is a fountain of fire—in the measure that it bubbles up, it inflames the thirsty soul. Love is the state of angels. Love is the progress of eternity. (*ibid*, Climacus; Sec. 35)

CHAPTER 13: How the Sacramental Christian Participates in the Fullness of the Triune Godhead

The Masoretic text of the Hebrew Bible refers to wisdom as "Chokhmah" (חָכְמָה). In the Septuagint (Transl. LXX), wisdom is "Sophia" (σοφία) and in the Vulgate it is "Sapientia." Roman Catholics refer to spiritual understanding in terms of their resultantly associated emotional elation known as Consolation (*Spiritual Exercises;* Ignatius of Loyola; Sec. 316; 1524).

However, divine wisdom was God's omniscient tool in creating life and the universe and it dwelt with God alone (Proverbs 8:22-31; Sirach 24:4; Wisdom 9:9-10). It was not available to people without His giving it (Job 28:12-13, 20-1, 23-27). Although God had "found" wisdom for Himself (Baruch 3:29-37), He nevertheless *gave* Chokhmah to Israel:

> He hath found out all the way of knowledge, and hath given it unto Jacob his servant, and to Israel His beloved. Afterward did He shew himself upon earth, and conversed with men. (Baruch 3:36-37)

Seeking wisdom for its own sake does not honor God; wisdom can only rightly be honored *in* God, as it says in this Apocryphal book:

> Wisdom shall praise her own self and shall be honored in God, and shall glory in the midst of her people. (Sirach 24:1-12)

CHAPTER 13: *How the Sacramental Christian Participates in the Fullness of the Triune Godhead*

The Narrow Gate will see far fewer people saved (Luke 13:23-24) compared to the *many* who, entering through the Wide Gate, sought wisdom as their end, instead of praying for the wisdom that the omnibenevolent God gives freely and abundantly (James 1:5):

> However, as Many have received salvation without prophecies and lights, without signs and wonders; but without humility no one will enter the marriage chamber. (*ibid*, Climacus; Step 25; Sec. 52)

Theoria built on the wisdom of the Logos, Who is Love, should also be enjoyably understood in light of what Clement of Alexandria wrote in his *Stromata*, the literary sources for which included the canonical books of Proverbs and Job.

Theoria, as Clement put it in the extended passage below, must be cultivated through the inspired listening and gazing of the heart toward the Word, and in so relishing the Liturgy, always receiving the Love of Fellowship in the Church— all of which help propagate divine wisdom for the soul.

Clement's words will be printed as the first of other passages that will seem unusually long for this chapter, but their significance is doubly important here: They characterize *theoria* at Mass time, and they also contemplate an Eastern

CHAPTER 13: How the Sacramental Christian Participates in the Fullness of the Triune Godhead

prayer form that could be modified and adapted for the Traditional Anglican Church. The following is what Clement wrote about harvesting *theoria*:

> But the husbandry is twofold—the one unwritten, and the other written. And in whatever way the Lord's labourer sow the good wheat, and grow and reap the ears, he shall appear a truly divine husbandman. Labour, says the Lord, not for the meat which perishes, but for that which endures to everlasting life [John 6:27]. And nutriment is received both by bread and by words. And truly blessed are the peace-makers [Matthew 5:9], who instructing those who are at war in their life and errors here, lead them back to the peace which is in the Word, and nourish for the life which is according to God, by the distribution of the bread, those that hunger after righteousness. For each soul has its own proper nutriment; some growing by knowledge and science, and others feeding on the Hellenic philosophy, the whole of which, like nuts, is not eatable. And he that plants and he that waters, being ministers of Him that gives the increase, are one in the ministry. But every one shall receive his own reward, according to his own work. For we are God's husbandmen, God's husbandry. You are God's building [1 Corinthians 3:8-9]

CHAPTER 13: *How the Sacramental Christian Participates in the Fullness of the Triune Godhead*

according to the Apostle. Wherefore the hearers are not permitted to apply the test of comparison. Nor is the word, given for investigation, to be committed to those who have been reared in the arts of all kinds of words, and in the power of inflated attempts at proof; whose minds are already preoccupied, and have not been previously emptied. But whoever chooses to banquet on faith, is steadfast for the reception of the divine words, having acquired already faith as a power of judging, according to reason. Hence ensues to him persuasion in abundance. And this was the meaning of that saying of prophecy, If you believe not, neither shall you understand [Isaiah 7:9]. As, then, we have opportunity, let us do good to all, especially to the household of faith [Galatians 6:10] And let each of these, according to the blessed David, sing, giving thanks. You shall sprinkle me with hyssop, and I shall be cleansed. You shall wash me, and I shall be whiter than the snow. You shall make me to hear gladness and joy, and the bones which have been humbled shall rejoice. Turn Your face from my sins. Blot out mine iniquities. Create in me a clean heart, O God, and renew a right spirit in my inward parts. Cast me not away from Your face, and take not Your Holy Spirit from me. Restore to

CHAPTER 13: How the Sacramental Christian Participates in the Fullness of the Triune Godhead

> me the joy of Your salvation, and establish me with Your princely spirit. (*The Stromata, or Miscellanies*; Saint Clement of Alexandria; Book II; Chapter I: Preface—The Author's Object—The Utility of Written Compositions"; A.D. 215)

The scientific mind should take note that Clement did **not** attribute the source of wisdom to Platonic solids or to the monad, as his beloved Plato did.[11] Nor is the *theoria* that is revealed to the human heart during the Christian Mass an "Ennead" that emanates from Sophia (as Clement's favorite Neoplatonist, Plotinus, had labeled such projections). Clement, in using the term, "gnosis," is not a Gnostic but is an Orthodox Christian careful to give the *pleroma* of the Triune Godhead all the credit:

> "Be not elated on account of your wisdom", say the Proverbs. "In all your ways acknowledge her, that she may direct your

---

[11] "Clement of Alexandria, a Christian Platonist, came to conversion through philosophy. In a series of allusive writings he presented a Hellenized Christianity along with the philosophical syncretism of his age: Stoic ethics, Aristotelian logic and especially Platonic metaphysics.... Clement's fusion of Platonism and Christianity vehemently opposed the dualism and determinism of gnostic theosophy, and stressed free choice and responsibility as fundamental to moral values" (*Clement of Alexandria (AD 150-215)*, Henry Chadwick, Routledge Encyclopedia of Philosophy, 1998).

CHAPTER 13: How the Sacramental Christian Participates in the Fullness of the Triune Godhead

ways, and that your foot may not stumble [Proverbs 3:5-6]"... You have, in brief, the professed aim of our philosophy; and the learning of these branches, when pursued with right course of conduct, leads through Wisdom, the artificer of all things, to the Ruler of all—a Being difficult to grasp and apprehend, ever receding and withdrawing from him who pursues. But He who is far off has—oh ineffable marvel!—come very near. I am a God that draws near, says the Lord. He is in essence remote; for how is it that what is begotten can have approached the Unbegotten? But He is very near in virtue of that power which holds all things in its embrace. Shall one do anything in secret, and I see him not? [Jeremiah 23:23-24] For the power of God is always present, in contact with us, in the exercise of inspection, of beneficence, of instruction. Whence Moses, persuaded that God is not to be known by human wisdom, said, Show me Your glory; [Exodus 33:18] and into the thick darkness where God's voice was, pressed to enter—that is, into the inaccessible and invisible ideas respecting Existence. For God is not in darkness or in place, but above both space and time, and qualities of objects. Wherefore neither is He at any time in a part, either as containing or as contained, either by

CHAPTER 13: *How the Sacramental Christian Participates in the Fullness of the Triune Godhead*

> limitation or by section. For what house will you build to Me? says the Lord. Isaiah 66:1 Nay, He has not even built one for Himself, since He cannot be contained. And though Heaven be called His throne, not even thus is He contained, but He rests delighted in the creation. (*ibid*, Clement; Chapter 2: "The Knowledge of God Can Be Attained Only Through Faith")

The *Catechetical Lectures* of Saint Cyril of Jerusalem explains how the liturgical celebrations of Baptism and the Eucharist provide occasions of spiritual direction for newcomers and the experienced alike to deepen their experience of prayer through both the sacraments and a daily re-offering of themselves to God. For Anglicans, the Daily Office, Ordinals, Feasts, and Fasts of the revisions of the Book of Common Prayer up until 1928 give the dependable Western verbal Form.

It is intended for orthodoxy to improve the interior life of the parishioner by comparing his human ontology with that of Jesus, during the Liturgy. In the Divine Liturgy of Saint John Chrysostom, it is warned that the Eucharist must be given only to a people set apart. During the Elevation of the Eucharist, as it is directed in Cyril's lectures (which structured the Liturgy of Saint James the Just), whereof the priest says,

CHAPTER 13: How the Sacramental Christian Participates in the Fullness of the Triune Godhead

"Be attentive! Holy things are for the holy!," the congregation replies, "One is Holy, One is the Lord, Jesus Christ." Saint Cyril noted:

> For One is truly holy, by nature holy; we too are holy, but not by nature, only by participation, and discipline, and prayer. (*Catechetical Lectures*; Saint Cyril of Jerusalem; Lec.23: On the Sacred Liturgy and Communion; A.D 345)

It is rewarding to acknowledge the catholicity between ancient orthodox liturgies. The proposition that the Antiochene Liturgy, the Jerusalem Liturgy of Saint Jerusalem, and that of Saint Ambrose could have been written or chiefly influenced by Cyril was originally predicated by the nineteenth-century theologian, Ferdinand Probst. He wrote that the Confession/Remission of sins occurring before the Our Father in these three liturgies was emphatically called for in Cyril's catechism (*ibid*, Cyril; Chap. 23; Sec. 11). He said that Saint Ambrose had noted the similarities between the rites:

> You hear that every time a sacrifice is offered, the death of the Lord, the resurrection of the Lord, the elevation of the Lord, and the remission of sins are signified. (*De Sacramentis;* Saint Ambrose of Milan; Book I; Chap. 5; Sec. 4; A.D. 380). Among the ancient liturgies, all of them, but especially

CHAPTER 13: How the Sacramental Christian Participates in the Fullness of the Triune Godhead

> the Coptic [catechetical] liturgy of Cyril, possess such an oration. The interpretation of the above words, confirmed by the ancient liturgies, therefore recommends the assumption that *exomologesis* [remission of sins] was a part of the old Milanese [Ambrosian] Mass. (*Liturgie des vierten jahrhunderts und deren reform;* Ferdinand Probst; Sec. 68; pp. 261-262; Aschendorff: Münster, 1893)

For Anglicans, choice over modes of contemplation that can supplement the Liturgy in one's personal hours can be left to the parishioner (if these choices fall within the Anglican Formularies). Whereas the mystical comprehension of *theoria* at Mass proceeds through the *Comfortable Words* and then initiates the *Anaphora* with the *Sanctus* of the Eucharistic Liturgy every Sunday morning, it is an open question as to whether supererogation (i.e., doing more than what God requires) would be taking place if the parishioner should take such additional contemplative steps to perform soulful emptying (i.e., *kenosis*), thereby taking care passively to render himself more available to the Grace of God's *Actus Purus* (i.e., His absolute perfection).

In preparing for the Mass, however, such supplementation could provide a spiritual

CHAPTER 13: How the Sacramental Christian Participates in the Fullness of the Triune Godhead

readiness beyond what the *Daily Office*, the *General Confession,* and the *Prayer for Humble Access* already impel. Then again—it may be contested by some—surely God's Grace is sufficient to bring about spiritual through the Mass in the 1928 *Book of Common Prayer.*

However, considering that so many have come to the Anglican Church through a wide variety of different Faith Traditions, it may be that a parishioner's heart may peacefully desire a broader range of licit ecclesiastical options for giving himself over to God. The Father searches the soul of a Christian 24 hours per day intending to make it spotless, and his tongue less deceiving of itself and others (Psalm 139:23-24), giving wisdom abundantly without upbraiding (James 1:5), and inspiring the Faithful to pursue a religion that is "pure and undefiled" (James 1:26-27).

Why would anyone seek intensive additional prayerful remediation beyond what the Canon already offers, except perhaps to adapt one's *kenosis* more readily for the arrival of God's Grace at the altar? Should it not be God's work alone to prepare the human mind and body for *theoria*?

For the West, it has always been via the Augustinian contention that the combination of God's Grace plus the choosing to live morally

CHAPTER 13: How the Sacramental Christian Participates in the Fullness of the Triune Godhead

brings about a peaceful existence (*Retractions*; Saint Augustine of Hippo; Book II; Chapter 66: On Grace and Free Will; Sec. 7: "Grace is Necessary Along with Free Will to Lead a Good Life"; A.D. 427).

However, at least according to the Aristotelian concept of *theikos praxis* of the Prime Mover, the doings of God have never needed to be incentivized by a communicant who conditionally promises God that he will see to it that his Faith shall shine forth by his employing new spiritual exercises in return for divine receipt of the *esse ipsum subsistens* (i.e., the essence of God being supplied through a subsistent act of His existence).

However, it leaves the choice in God's mind so long as the will to volunteer unsolicited "extra-credit homework" is an act of Love.

Thus, it would be an act of Love for the communicant to ask God to work through him during his increased prayer works for the purpose of gaining practical understanding about how best to serve God with the sincerest Agape of heart, soul, and mind:

> Jesus said unto him, Thou shalt love the Lord thy God with all thy heart, and with all thy soul, and with all thy mind. This is

CHAPTER 13: How the Sacramental Christian Participates in the Fullness of the Triune Godhead

> the first and great commandment.
> (Matthew 22:37)

The applied ancient term is *phronema* (*Nichomachean Ethics;* Aristotle; Book VI; Sec: 1140-a,b; 1142), which basically means to learn and know all the reasons why one needs to be virtuous. It is the celestial wisdom of *Spiritual Discernment* that moves a person to derive necessary means to comprehend Logos through the Liturgy, the Law of Moses, Absolute Truth, and Objective Morality. It is, in a sense, to learn to *think* like Christ.

> For who hath known the mind of the Lord, that he may instruct him? but we have the mind of Christ. (1 Corinthians 2:16)

Here is another example of what some could consider supererogation. The term "daily bread" in the Lord's Prayer is alternately literally translated from the Greek (*epiousios*) as "super-substantial bread." What if the Christian, in an attempt to follow exactly "Thy will be done" sought to eat this precious bread every day?

Hence, if it were allowed in one's parish, could not the Eucharist be eaten every day, if the priest, discerning that the practice served *Agape* in the heart of the mindful, allowed it?

> Give us this day our substantial bread. This common bread is not substantial bread, but

> this Holy Bread is substantial, that is, appointed for the substance of the soul. For this Bread goes not into the belly and is cast out into the draught [Matthew 15:17], but is distributed into your whole system for the benefit of body and soul. But by this day, He means, each day, as also Paul said, While it is called today [Hebrews 3:15]. (*ibid*, Cyril; Lec. 23)

This explains why many Roman Catholics are daily communicants. Those who don't understand what they are doing might believe they are engaging in supererogation when in reality they may believe they are more closely aligning themselves to the will of God by communicating with Him in the Eucharist daily.

Moreover, being that the contemplative person merely loves to send up prayers and gain consolation, and so, also, the sincere humble performing of the "**Jesus Prayer**," or *Hesychasm*, would never be a labor of superfluous or heretical "works righteousness," or supererogation, because the goal of *theoria* is Agape, as described by Climacus above.

And yet, *Hesychasm* would appear to adapt to a different modality of ecclesiology (e.g., Eastern) that is at best pure and undefiled, but one that is not developed for Traditional Anglicans

CHAPTER 13: How the Sacramental Christian Participates in the Fullness of the Triune Godhead

normally to follow. Could it not be modified or adapted?

The writings of Saint Gregory of Palamas offer much beauty to aid the contemplative life of the Christian, and thus they are reserved as a personal choice for the individual Anglican communicant whether to practice additional scriptural forms of contemplation, contrition, and penitential acts, to benefit his or her spirituality and to help ready the soul for Fellowship with the Triune Godhead at the altar.

CHAPTER 13: How the Sacramental Christian Participates in the Fullness of the Triune Godhead

By the Jesus Prayer or in practicing *Hesychasm*, practitioners seek divine quietness through their contemplation of God in uninterrupted, repeated recitation of the following simple prayer: Lord Jesus Christ, Son of God, have mercy on me, a sinner.[12]

Recitation of the Jesus Prayer, often with the use of prayer beads, is a meditative technique whose brevity does not have to be copied. Such a prayer can be embellished during one's regular day using many other Scripture-based prayers. For example, one could say: "Lord, I believe; help thou mine unbelief" (Mark 9:24).

It was the great striving by Saint John Cassian (who was both ordained and protected by Chrysostom) who made famous the teachings of his mentor, Evagrius Ponticus (the father of eremitic monasticism), for whom Cassian wrote the *Conferences*. The vibrant conversations collected in this book offer means for a Christian to overcome the "Eight Evil Temptations" that Ponticus had described in the *Logismoi*. Cassian prescribed *Hesychasm* to help the sinner cope using a self-soothing means of luring his mind away from error by repeating the Jesus Prayer to resist evil:

---

[12] There are several variations of the Jesus Prayer, but this one is the most common.

CHAPTER 13: *How the Sacramental Christian Participates in the Fullness of the Triune Godhead*

> I am affected by the passion of gluttony... I am incited to anticipate the hour fixed for supper, or I am trying with great sorrow of heart to keep to the limits of the right and regular meagre fare. I must cry out with groans: O God, make speed to save me: O Lord, make haste to help me... In order that effect may be given to my wishes, or else that the fire of carnal lust may be quenched without the remedy of a stricter fast, I must pray: O God, make speed to save me: O Lord, make haste to help me. .. I feel that the incentive to lust is removed, and that the heat of passion has died away in my members: In order that this good condition acquired, or rather that this grace of God may continue still longer or forever with me, I must earnestly say: O God, make speed to save me: O Lord, make haste to help me. I am disturbed by the pangs of anger, covetousness, gloominess, and driven to disturb the peaceful state in which I was, and which was dear to me: In order that I may not be carried away by raging passion into the bitterness of gall, I must cry out with deep groans: O God, make speed to save me: O Lord, make haste to help me. (*Conferences*; Saint John Cassian; Conf. 10: "Method of Continual Prayer"; A.D. 420)

CHAPTER 13: How the Sacramental Christian Participates in the Fullness of the Triune Godhead

The distinction between the essence (*ousia*) and the energies (*energeia*) of God were explained simply by Saint John of Damascus: All that can be affirmed epistemologically about God manifests not His nature but the things *about* His nature (*An Exposition of the Orthodox Faith;* Saint John of Damascus; Book I; Chapter 4: "Concerning the Nature of Deity: That it is Incomprehensible."; d. A.D. 749).

God's *pleroma* at the altar, therefore, cannot be experienced in terms of its overwhelming *energy* but in the safe *essence* of His omnipresence.

Therefore, the *energy* and *essence* of God can be comprehended through God's association with the altar in how the "energy" of His Grace substantiates the Body and Blood during the Divine Liturgy (*ibid*, Damascus; Book IV; Chapter 13).

While this gives the spirituality of Eastern Orthodoxy a place within the Anglican *via media*, it also offers fertile ground for future ecumenical dialogues on the subject.

In the meantime, if an Anglican wishes humbly to engage the *noetic* (i.e., intellect) in order to produce, say, an act of contrition by which God could sanctify the mind with humility, then his heart must, as always, be happily willing to suffer agonizing deprivation against the shadow of his resisted concupiscence, as his soul awaits Sunday, when God's mercy will produce the *theoria* in Fellowship with other communicants during the *anaphora*. Palamas wrote:

> Because the Deity is goodness itself, true mercy and an abyss of loving bounty—or, rather, He is that which embraces and contains this abyss, since He transcends every name that is named [Ephesians 1:21] and everything we can conceive—we can receive mercy only by union with Him. We unite ourselves to Him, in so far as this is possible, by participating in the godlike virtues and by entering into communion with Him through prayer and praise. Because the virtues are similitudes of God, to participate in them puts us in a fit state to receive the Deity, yet it does not actually unite us to Him. But prayer through its sacral and hieratic power actualizes our ascent to and union with the Deity, for it is a bond between noetic creatures and their Creator. Or at least this happens when our prayer, through its fervent compunction, transcends the passions and conceptual thoughts; for the intellect, while still passion-dominated, cannot be united to God. Thus so long as the intellect when praying remains in a passion-charged state, it will not obtain mercy; but to the extent that it can dispel distractive

CHAPTER 13: How the Sacramental Christian Participates in the Fullness of the Triune Godhead

> thoughts it will experience inward grief, and in so far as it experiences such grief it will partake of God's mercy. And if with humility it continues to savour this mercy, it will transform entirely the aspect of the soul that is accessible to passion. (*Philokalia*; Saint Gregory of Palamas; "Three Texts on Prayer and Purity of Heart"; Sec. 1; A.D. 1350)

The fourteenth article of the *Thirty-Nine Articles of Religion* disqualifies the merit of supererogation unless the activity with an attitude of humility (i.e., "We are unprofitable servants"), because holy examples remain holy so long as "we have done that which was our duty to do" (Luke 17:10).

Therefore, if a person operating within the *via media* came with true humble Faith to desire to practice *Hesychasm,* or to receive the Eucharist daily, he is not serving pride or engaging in supererogation. Rather, he may believe that receiving in oneself daily the *epiousios* (i.e., the "super-substantial bread") was a literal command of the Lord in the Lord's Prayer, as explicated by Saint Cyprian of Carthage (quoted at the end of this chapter).

The Customary of a Traditional Anglican church may indulge peaceful, humble requests that exceed conventional expectations—for example, if the priest is willing to supply the Eucharist

CHAPTER 13: *How the Sacramental Christian Participates in the Fullness of the Triune Godhead*

every day and, as with *Hesychasm,* tolerate organized valid contemplative prayer forms within his Parish—but may not *mandate* daily Communion or the formation of a society that demands a certain type of praying that is not part of the Anglican tradition.

The words and examples of the catholic orthodox Anglican worshiper should at any rate always retain the tradition of emanating selfless Love among the Faithful so as not to create a stumbling block:

> Let us not therefore judge one another any more: but judge this rather, that no man put a stumblingblock or an occasion to fall in his brother's way. (Romans 14:13)

Cyprian, the Bishop of Carthage, explicated that "our daily bread" is meant both literally and spiritually. It so happens that he came down on the side of literally communicating with Christ in the Eucharist daily:

> As the prayer goes forward, we ask and say, Give us this day our daily bread. And this may be understood both spiritually and literally, because either way of understanding it is rich in divine usefulness to our salvation. For Christ is the bread of life; and this bread does not belong to all men, but it is ours. And according as we say, Our Father,

CHAPTER 13: How the Sacramental Christian Participates in the Fullness of the Triune Godhead

because He is the Father of those who understand and believe; so also we call it our bread, because Christ is the bread of those who are in union with His body. And we ask that this bread should be given to us daily, that we who are in Christ, and daily receive the Eucharist for the food of salvation, may not, by the interposition of some heinous sin, by being prevented, as withheld and not communicating, from partaking of the heavenly bread, be separated from Christ's body, as He Himself predicts, and warns, I am the bread of life which came down from heaven. If any man eat of my bread, he shall live for ever: and the bread which I will give is my flesh, for the life of the world. John 6:58 When, therefore, He says, that whoever shall eat of His bread shall live for ever; as it is manifest that those who partake of His body and receive the Eucharist by the right of communion are living, so, on the other hand, we must fear and pray lest any one who, being withheld from communion, is separate from Christ's body should remain at a distance from salvation; as He Himself threatens, and says, Unless you eat the flesh of the Son of man, and drink His blood, you shall have no life in you. John 6:53 And therefore we ask that our bread—that is, Christ—may be given to us daily, that we who

CHAPTER 13: How the Sacramental Christian Participates in the Fullness of the Triune Godhead

abide and live in Christ may not depart from His sanctification and body. (*Treatises on the Lord's Prayer;* Saint Cyprian of Carthage; Part 18; d. A.D. 258)

CHAPTER 14: Aristotelian and Thomasian Hylomorphism Emboldens Attempts by the Lukewarm to Overlap Science & Metaphysics

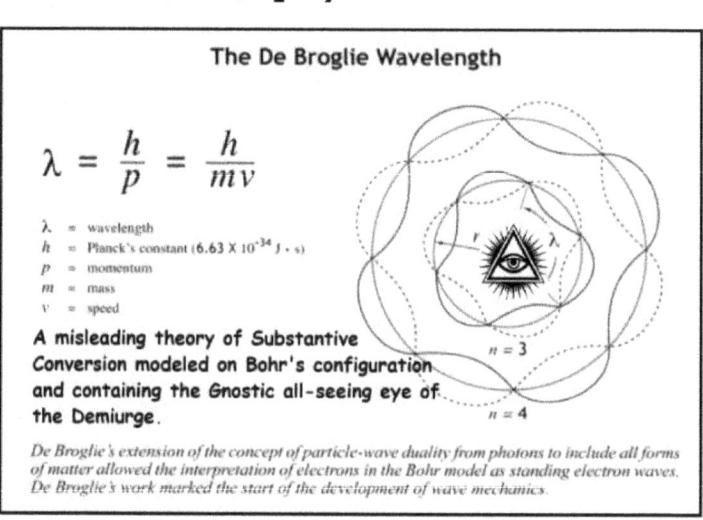

Proving Transubstantiation happens is given the "ol' college try" within science, as well. Never since the Belgian priest Fr. Georges Lemaître derived calculations from General Relativity that led him to the *Big Bang Theory* has there been so much interest in trying to use science to prove what is happening at the Roman Catholic altar.

Certain physicists, conceptualizing that the conversion of bread and wine is a "spatiotemporal arrangement of microscopic constituents," theorize that they have opened a path toward a "non-reductive conception" of

CHAPTER 14: *Aristotelian and Thomasian Hylomorphism Emboldens Attempts by the Lukewarm to Overlap Science & Metaphysics*

nature familiar to the presumptions of thinkers such as Saint Thomas Aquinas and Aristotle, who pondered the idea of *hylomorphism* (*From Quantum Physics to Classical Metaphysics*; William M.R. Simpson; Neo-Aristotelian Metaphysics and the Theology of Nature; pp. 21-65; Routledge: 2021).

Hylomorphism is the concept that, implied within the physical Matter of every object and person is the Form of its perfect state or outcome (*Metaphysics*; Aristotle; Chapter 11; Part 9; A.D. 350; and *Comments on* Metaphysics; Saint Thomas Aquinas; Book 8; Chapters 8-9; 1270).

Physicists attempt to draw ontological conclusions from humanists interested only in physically observable data instead of spiritual discernment, painting bleak premises such as the perusal by a philosopher/microphysicalist:

> ...all there is to the world is a vast mosaic of local matters of particular fact, just one little thing and then another... We have geometry: a system of external relations of spatio-temporal distances between points... And at those points we have local qualities: perfectly natural intrinsic properties which need nothing bigger than a point at which to be instantiated. For short, we have an arrangement of qualities. And that is all. *(On*

CHAPTER 14: *Aristotelian and Thomasian Hylomorphism Emboldens Attempts by the Lukewarm to Overlap Science & Metaphysics*

the Plurality of Worlds; David Lewis; Blackwell Philosophy; P. ix; Oxford: 1986)

Regarding the Eucharist, the parallel idea would be that the ultimate or perfect Form implied by bread, wine, Jesus, or people would somehow be contained in their ordinary Matter and thus can be quantified. That is, people and things would have to gain the measurable data of a quantifiable essence or energy God existing in human design, as if science could prove how heavenly perfection becomes instantiated by a person's or a thing's existential denouement! It is impossible because God is too great to be quantified (*Proslogion*; Chapter 15; Saint Anselm of Canterbury; 1078).

To produce itself as a quantifiable conversion of God's Real Presence into "a basic notion of substance," Transubstantiation must have a "thick, central role in organizing the science of Metaphysics" (*Substance Made Manifest: Metaphysical and Semantic Implications of the Doctrine of Transubstantiation;* Joshua Hochschild; Saint Anselm Journal; Issue 2; Vol 9; pp. 1-21; 2014).

In other words, physicists must propose that while ordinary objects such as bread possess the Form that determines the nature firstly of "loaf Matter" that becomes "God Matter," their atoms

CHAPTER 14: Aristotelian and Thomasian Hylomorphism Emboldens Attempts by the Lukewarm to Overlap Science & Metaphysics

should somehow be affected by, say, Quantum Entanglement to produce the Conversion of bread and wine into the Body and Blood of God. Or, they would have to argue, that it is not through what they call *microphysicalism* (i.e., the nitty gritty of quantum particle movement and hence their signatures measured precisely) but from the perspective of *macroscopic* phenomena so that, at least in a broad sense, they can comprehend how Transubstantiation works.

Lately it has been proposed that God is merely transubstantiated as a hologram, in order to devise a quantum-mechanical theory of the Eucharist in light of the principle that His essence is encoded in the lower dimension of consumable matter. By these metaphysics it is argued:

> ...how the concept of religious covenant justifies the 'law' of transubstantiation because both exemplify how the Transcendent is historically and literally present—a 'doubling' we see in quantum superposition. (*Transubstantiation and Quantum Mechanical Theory;* Mark P. Fusco; Chapter 6: "The Physics and Metaphysics of Transubstantiation"; pp. 221-245; London, Palgrave Macmillan, Cham.: 2023)

CHAPTER 14: Aristotelian and Thomasian Hylomorphism Emboldens Attempts by the Lukewarm to Overlap Science & Metaphysics

According to Jesuit priest, Fr. Mark P. Fusco, the mathematical "proof" of quantum entanglement helps frame this "holo-cryptic" argument concerning the substantiation of the Host, whereas the prospects of accident, chance, uncertainty, and randomness would also "subtract" or reduce the possibility that one is absolutely certain about one's observations (*ibid*, Fusco).

> This scientific theory for representing physical matter's identity is recognized, for example, in the symmetry existing between a subatomic particle and its orbital shell, a single particle's identity in relationship to its thermodynamic system, Hawking radiation, and black hole entropy. Further, the properties of quantum non-locality and teleportation signpost a new way to understand the Eternal Logos' relationship to Jesus Christ and the Eucharist. (*ibid*, Fusco)

Thus presumably the unseeable conversion into the Body and Blood becomes adaptable to the psyche by way of:

> Holo-cryptic metaphysics [which] sees in the so-called [John Stewart] Bell's inequalities [in his mathematical defense of quantum entanglement], non-locality, quantum teleportation, and David Bohm's implicate

CHAPTER 14: Aristotelian and Thomasian Hylomorphism Emboldens Attempts by the Lukewarm to Overlap Science & Metaphysics

> order a means to justify a theological reading of the holographic symmetry existing between Jesus Christ and the Eucharist. (*ibid*, Fusco)

This projection of Jesus Christ's place in history and within the anaphora is taken by Fusco in light of God's presence having "Absolute Groundless" relevance to the physicist, in that Faith lacks substantial scientific evidence or justification of His existence aside from the Logos which can better yet be spiritually discerned, and yet also affirmed as purporting itself to be a hologram (*ibid,* Fusco).

Ethereal "data," however, cannot be broken down into "finite temperature quantum systems" (observing the changes on the paten and in the cup, and theorizing as to why whatever is visible under an electron microscope actually has a seeable or unseeable wave or spin attached to it that signifies perfection, or God).

Physicists further contemplate Hylomorphism via the Broglie-Bohm theory,[13] by which a single "cosmic substance"—perhaps a soul or a Prime Mover, against whose supreme irresistible Form any lesser quantum configurations can

---

[13] That is, that quantum particles with unique wave functions exist that can never be observed but nevertheless should be presumed to exist.

CHAPTER 14: Aristotelian and Thomasian Hylomorphism Emboldens Attempts by the Lukewarm to Overlap Science & Metaphysics

ultimately (and happily) be subsumed into its oneness according to the nature of its higher Form—can become substantiated by the power of God into the lesser realm of perceivable existence. All that would be needed is a priest—who "gets" science!

In other words, in this view, the priest as the "metaphysicist" would somehow be performing Transubstantiation by invoking the Will of the Creator to instantiate into the corporeality of bread and wine that are tasted among mortals His objective eînai (εἶναι of that "I am").

They admit that they merely do not know *how* the conversion takes place, or *how* to quantify it, but that it in some way belongs to the wave or spin of quanta that are necessarily always paradoxically perceivable as the polar opposites of what can be mathematically measured or instrumentally witnessed. And so their attempts to correlate science with metaphysics invariably play off more like Gnostic hunches and postulations about the Demiurge and the "perfect realm" of Forms (i.e., *hyperouranos*), with technical terms thrown in, than Traditional Christianity (*ibid*, Simpson).

For those curious about Eastern Orthodoxy, Saint Gregory of Palamas may have already arrived at something *like* the Broglie-Bohm theory of a

CHAPTER 14: *Aristotelian and Thomasian Hylomorphism Emboldens Attempts by the Lukewarm to Overlap Science & Metaphysics*

hylomorphically perceived Incarnation, and other phenomena, beating modern scientific thought by about 700 years. To him, the *theosis*, which is the conjoining of the saved person with God, is where Salvation becomes a greater work than the Creation of the person. He did not use science falsely so called (1 Timothy 6:20), but employed metaphysics instead.

Thus for Palamas, at the Rapture, the same light of the Transfiguration transports the Elect—that is, both their physical bodies and their spirits—into the heavens, to join with God. The sinful works of pride, says Palamas, must be overcome in the meantime (to avoid microphysical entanglements of course) so that the "macro" of the Godhead can bring the saved person into Eternity. He posited:

> Take yourself in hand, then, be attentive to yourself, scrutinize yourself; or, rather, guard, watch over and test yourself, for in this manner you will subdue your rebellious unregenerate self to the Spirit and there will never again be "some secret iniquity in your heart" (Deuteronomy 15:9). (*Philokalia*; "Saint Gregory Palamas: In Defense of Those who Devoutly Practice a Life of Stillness"; Part 9; 1344)

CHAPTER 14: Aristotelian and Thomasian Hylomorphism Emboldens Attempts by the Lukewarm to Overlap Science & Metaphysics

As a Christian rule of thumb, mastering Quantum Mechanics would be a non-expedient (1 Corinthians 6:12) means of invoking or understanding the Real Presence at the altar. Combining the much simpler Liturgy in the 1928 *Book of Common Prayer* with good Priestly Intention and the loving Fellowship of the *ecclesia* are all the "math" any Anglican Christian needs—all that *any* Christian has ever needed for Substantiation to occur at the altar since the inception of Holy Communion in the Church.

Faith does not need science, correctly or falsely so called, to substantiate belief in the Real Presence, for it is the evidence of things not seen (Hebrews 11:1).

CHAPTER 15: Conclusion

It is in the spirit of loving Fellowship between Trinitarian churchgoers that the Eucharist—that is, the Body and Blood of Christ—may be shared and understood within the limitations of the psyche to be the Real Presence of Christ in a Paschal Mystery. The examples of William Laud, Richard Hooker, and the Eastern Orthodox theologians should always be remembered for the capacity of these men to lovingly preserve Sacred Tradition, which passes down these truths to us to the present day.

As a side note, dialogue between the Anglican Communion and the Eastern Orthodox ceased being relevant after the Moscow Conference of 1976—that is, until the birth of the Continuing and Traditional Anglican movement at the time of the Saint Louis Affirmation of 1978. Traditional Anglican jurisdictions do not collaborate in Ecumenical activity with the Anglican Communion, which they have ruled (since the Liturgical Revolution causing the 1978 and later dissentions) is an institution that has dedicated itself to profane and sordid uses. In contrast, eventual Communion between the Eastern and Western Orthodox Churches and the Traditional Anglican Church is a continuing aim of Fellowship conducted on the local, Metropolitan, Diocesan, and Parish levels.

CHAPTER 15: Conclusion

I wrote this book concerning the Substantiation of the Real Presence in the Eucharist while I was Reverend Canon of the Diocese of the Northeast of Traditional Anglican Church of America (TACA). This writing aims to provide sound catechetical teaching on the important subject of the Eucharist—not only by looking at Church history and metaphysics, but also by simply relating my own experience of coming into the Continuing-Anglican movement, bringing my whole family with me, and finding this TACA suitable for planting a church, and why.

To analyze the *via media* and Broad Church approach to *ecclesia* as it concerns the founding of a Traditionalist Christian home (in my case, Saint Patrick's Anglican Church), it is useful to detail why special "callings" to preside over the invocation of Real Presence must be considered in light of the examples known about the lives of the Jacobean and Carolingian churchmen William Laud and Richard Hooker, respectively; the Counter-Reformationist Jesuit Robert Bellarmine; and, for mere objective comparability, the Eucharistic catechesis of the Eastern Orthodox Church. The hope is that the reader will find the matter worthy of prayerful contemplation and further independent study.

CHAPTER 15: Conclusion

EPILOGUE: More About the Orthodox, but This Time, the Western Ones

And, as a coda to this piece, by what paths and byways did the author bring his family to the Traditional Anglican Church of America (TACA), and can our tale be understood according to the above material in a meaningful way?

We came to Traditional Anglicanism by way of a certain branch of the Moscow Patriarchate, where we had been rebaptized and Chrismated in a certain parish according to the rubrics of the Western Rite Orthodox Church, historically founded in the 1920s by Saint Mikhail Borisovich Maximovitch (a.k.a. Saint John of Shanghai and of San Francisco). We shall refer to this Church as "the Branch"; other than this particular parish within the Branch, the Patriarchate and the other parts of the Branch were populated by truly fine Christians, with whom I was happily acquainted. We would have been happier to befriend some of them for longer, truly. However, for eight months, we were faithful attendees at this parish, which had previously been an important worship site of the Episcopal Charismatic Church, but we did not realize until we found cause to research this origin of this weird congregation, the same charismatic members and their practices were still entirely present. Its ex-psychedelic members were indeed chrismated

EPILOGUE: More About the Orthodox, but This Time, the Western Ones

as Orthodox, and their leader had earned a Masters in Divinity (through a Bishop running a correspondence course). More will be said about them, shortly.

We had come to this parish by way of Traditionalist Catholicism, or Sedevacantism. In turn, we came to Sedevacantism by way of shedding ourselves of the Novus Ordo Liturgical Revolution, known as the modern Roman Catholic Church. This latter leviathan is where we had been baptized and confirmed, and where we ran an astonishingly successful nonprofit charitable ministry for six years, known as Catholic Philadelphia Outreach (CPO).

CPO thrived with hundreds of volunteers and had thousands of recipients of charity. After a while, most of the volunteers revealed themselves to be Marxist-/Liberal-minded, and they never wanted to participate in anything remotely touching religion except for charity. But as the hair color turned purple and green, and the "Hate Trump" ethos grew, it became increasingly difficult to explain that CPO's mission was to perform good works as an emanation of the Faith in Christ that increasingly few of them had. Ultimately, due to the abuses and shameful darkness of the Philadelphia Archdiocese, with certain of its priests and nuns who jealously upbraided or disgusted us, and all

EPILOGUE: More About the Orthodox, but This Time, the Western Ones

of its sodomite pedophile ministers who disturbed us, we agonizingly left, eventually joining the Branch.

In the Branch now, working with far fewer volunteers, all of them coming from a single church, we fared little better. We found ourselves coming up against the corrupt, mercurial Rector of this tiny but well-known church, a man who exploited us and our ministry while intending to oversee my postulancy as a seminarian to become grandfathered into ordination.

In the meanwhile, "Just apply," he assured me, to our "Oblate Society" and keep on studying "at" our correspondence-course seminary where the Rector's friend was still graduating people he thought were worthy.

We found ourselves malingering at a nominally Orthodox outfit that had imported into its services a patchwork quilt of parts of the 1928 *Book of Common Prayer* and the Sarum Rite, English translations of Chrysostom's Prokiemenon, the Doxologie, the Catechumens, the Eucharistic Anaphora, and an apostatic Charismatic laying of hands on Wednesday nights. They seemed at times ashamed that they used to talk in tongues, or that some of them had during youth consumed a lot of LSD, and they were hunted for money by the Rector, who

EPILOGUE: More About the Orthodox, but This Time, the Western Ones

said he was paranoid beyond our capacity for analysis about "the Vicar General coming up from Florida to close them down for not having perfectly functioning bathrooms!" As a side note, the Vicar was a kindly fellow who knew that he did not have the authority to shut down this fledgling church. However, the Rector still begged constantly for money from the same people every Sunday afternoon and then enjoyed coffee and cake while gossiping loudly about the people who had left his church.

The Oblate society was a reading group run by a laicized madwoman Roman Catholic plainclothes nun, an ex-Marine, who assigned readings by the self-help Christian-esque author Max Lucado. One time, she hounded me for not picking up her air conditioner to donate it to CPO on Thanksgiving. Another time, when I was sworn into the Oblates and received my shiny medallion, she jammed her thumb into my xyphoid because I had not quickly stood up during a prayer.

The Bishop who was running the "seminary" was a highly educated man but was known to be an infamous womanizer. He was concealing a non-canonical second marriage and was a disgruntled founding member of the Diocese (he was always upset about "the coup" that befell him some years back) but received a monthly stipend for

EPILOGUE: More About the Orthodox, but This Time, the Western Ones

his e-mail and telephone pedagogy. He had written the Liturgy and arranged the hymnary for the Branch—a highly gifted, ingenious, emotionally insecure elderly man with long grey hair, a white beard, and a gigantic chip on his shoulder.

The Rector gladly accepted approximately $3,500 from my wife and me over the course of about six months as tithes and gifts, and he readily welcomed for himself direct donations that had originally been given to CPO, no matter how small, before he was done with us. But he was still constantly begging for money from everyone by holding long coffee meetups at which he screened straight-talk prosperity-Gospel-oriented videos to prod his parishioners into priming their purses, assuring us that "charity comes back to you." When I began to accuse him of corruption, he put out that I was insane, and so I began to escape the emotional tethers of this operation by gradually lampooning the folly I was perceiving, until one day a local police detective phoned me at home to threaten me never to come near the "Very Reverend's" church again.

A year after we left this "Very Reverend" and his church, having moved about an hour and a half away from it, we found out that he died. He was only 72. His online memorials displayed several

EPILOGUE: More About the Orthodox, but This Time, the Western Ones

affectionate testimonials revealing the scandalous information that he had all along been living in a private home with a longtime male lover (even though he had repeatedly told his congregation that he was broke and was living perpetually alone in a state of near impoverishment). Once of the worst parts of the entire ordeal is that his inner circle knew all along about the man's double life.

It was reported a year after his death that after he died, the famous "streaming icon" (noted by the lacrimation from the eyes of the Theotokos of exceedingly fragrant oil) never again "cried." I recall seeing that the dark wooden back panel of this small painting was suitably voluminous to house batteries and a pump, but I never was able to test my hypothesis because the image was always held protectively by the Priest or concealed someplace between Liturgical hours.

The thought of this chicanery and betrayal grieves my heart to this day. Watching helplessly as men flirt with damnation because of their blasphemous desperation and sinful addictions causes me great sadness. Please help me keep this man in my prayers—for his soul and for those who loved him, protected him, and were influenced by him.

During our time in the Branch, my wife and I continued to contemplate what the flaw could

EPILOGUE: More About the Orthodox, but This Time, the Western Ones

possibly be within popular religion that inspired lunacy within the clergy. We detected error in, among a number of other things, the teaching of Transubstantiation and Consubstantiation, wherein the Real Presence is inflicted in a dogmatic way on the Faithful, as if the Salvation of the Communicants depended not only on "correct belief" in it, but also upon the supposed power of the priest. It is an example of heretical Gnosis, really.

It would take us a full decade to recognize the ways in which misunderstandings about the Eucharist are generally accompanied by disordered pastoral ideation and warped obeisance to the priest on the part of the laity. Believing that the priest has a special power that features a substantive variation in the bread and wine, the laity and other churchgoers either become his toadies or close one eye to his strangeness or abuses, or they accept it as a given that a serious intellectual flaw can help a psychologically challenged clergyman become megalomaniacal menace. That is, an ordained man may become convinced that he is a magician at the altar and in all walks of life—that is, if he wrongfully learns that the Real Presence moves only because he, the priest, is the mover.

EPILOGUE: More About the Orthodox, but This Time, the Western Ones

Transubstantiation is still enacted in most Apostolic churches, along with the Anglo-Catholic "cathedral" described at the beginning of this book. Its Permanently Interim Archbishop showed us early on how he worked to ensure that his followers could be put back into alignment with him theologically if they fell out. He was suddenly telling us during one fateful afternoon that he would not support us during an argument with an angry parishioner. The wrathful man, in mock indignation, was hostilely condoning his wife's attempt to drag my youngest son into the church cellar, to "show you some lovely things." I begged our exiled Bishop to intervene.

However, as he was a widower for 20 years, that turbulent couple were among the very few friends and parishioners he had left. He needed their tithes, and so he didn't oppose them; my head was spinning. This same minister had also asked us to keep mum about the covert girlfriend he would bring to coffee hour, the widow whose shoulders he publicly stroked while we sat around in a circle drinking coffee and eating donuts, all because he was needy and lonely and the world just would never understand.

EPILOGUE: More About the Orthodox, but This Time, the Western Ones

I believe that this particular Archbishop deserves to be granted the time to recognize the error of his ways, just as Abp. Laud eventually became meek and begged aloud for God's mercy.

I moved my family a few months after leaving that Orthodox church. I spent a year and half working feverishly on my new farm to forget my troubles, and praying for the strength to move on from all these people. Growing more analytical as my heavier emotions ebbed, I finally realized that what was missing from all these churches that enjoyed Apostolic Succession was simply the commitment by the pastor to really believe what was prayed and to act on that belief, but in a spirit of true humility.

It is to improve Fellowship with, and to educate, my readers that I have related all these things. Most especially, I have written this book for the next generation—for the children who will grow up in the Anglican Church—so that these cautionary tales are not lost to history. From generation to generation it is our duty to teach the proper understanding of the Holy Eucharist.

Please pray that God makes me into a better father, husband, priest, and friend so that by the grace of God I can continue to carry out the ministry to which I was called.

EPILOGUE: More About the Orthodox, but This Time, the Western Ones

God bless you and yours.

Bishop Michael DellaVecchia (at the time of this writing, in May 2024, being Reverand Canon) of the Northeast Diocese of Traditional Anglican Church of America, and the Rector of Saint Patrick's Anglican Church.

###

APPENDIX A: The Bible is the True Source of the Traditional Anglican Mass — A Biblical Sacramental Reference Guide

From Genesis to Revelation the Anglican liturgies of the Word and of the Eucharist are always the product of Sacred Scripture. They have never strayed from the Word of God. Appendix A, a reference guide, serves to compile and explain the many verses that substantiate the sections of the Holy Communion Mass of the *1928 Book of Common Prayer.*

Throughout this guide, the Mass is identified by its sections or topics in bold capital print. The verse from the King James Bible will fall below it. Finally, instructive commentary, as applicable, will occur in italics.

It is important to note here that the order of the following definitions is *not* chronological, meaning it is not presented in the same order as would occur in the Liturgy. Instead, topics are organized in terms of how holy meditation might correlate one element of the Mass to another, approaching the way that contemplation during soulful prayer tends to navigate itself for optimal comprehension. Let us begin:

APPENDIX A: The Bible Is the True Source of the Traditional Anglican Mass - A Biblical Sacramental Reference Guide

THE *ANAPHORA* OR EUCHARISTIC PRAYER

And as they were eating, Jesus took bread, and blessed it, and brake it, and gave it to the disciples, and said, Take, eat; this is my body. (Matthew 26:26)

THE *ANAMNESIS* OF THE ETERNAL MEMORY

For I say unto you, I will not drink of the fruit of the vine, until the kingdom of God shall come. And He took bread, and gave thanks, and brake it, and gave unto them, saying, This is my body which is given for you: this do in remembrance of me. Likewise also the cup after supper, saying, This cup is the new testament in my blood, which is shed for you. (Luke 22:18-20)

The cup of blessing which we bless, is it not the communion of the blood of Christ? The bread which we break, is it not the communion of the body of Christ? For we being many are one bread, and one body: for we are all partakers of that one bread. (1 Corinthians 10:16-17)

For the bread of God is he which cometh down from heaven, and giveth life unto the world. Then said they unto him, Lord, evermore give us this bread. And Jesus said unto them, I am the bread of life: he that cometh to me shall never hunger; and he that believeth on me shall never thirst. (John 6:33-35)

APPENDIX A: The Bible Is the True Source of the Traditional Anglican Mass – A Biblical Sacramental Reference Guide

> And as they did eat, Jesus took bread, and blessed, and brake it, and gave to them, and said, Take, eat: this is my body. And He took the cup, and when He had given thanks, He gave it to them: and they all drank of it. And He said unto them, This is my blood of the new testament, which is shed for many. Verily I say unto you, I will drink no more of the fruit of the vine, until that day that I drink it new in the kingdom of God. (Mark 14:22-25)

CONFESSION: THAT FREEDOM FROM UNTRUTH IS NECESSARY TO PURGE FAITHLESSNESS

> If we confess our sins, He is faithful and just to forgive us our sins and to cleanse us from all unrighteousness. (1 John 1:9)

> Beware lest any man spoil you through philosophy and vain deceit, after the tradition of men, after the rudiments of the world, and not after Christ. (Colossians 2:8)

> And ye have not His word abiding in you: for whom He hath sent, Him ye believe not. Search the scriptures; for in them ye think ye have eternal life: and they are they which testify of me. And ye will not come to me, that ye might have life. (John 5:38-40)

All doubts must be dispelled so that Fellowship with Christ may commence and Revelation be attained because Christ intends to indwell within the hearts of the saved Elect.

APPENDIX A: The Bible Is the True Source of the Traditional Anglican Mass – A Biblical Sacramental Reference Guide

> Your glorying is not good. Know ye not that a little leaven leaveneth the whole lump? Purge out therefore the old leaven, that ye may be a new lump, as ye are unleavened. For even Christ our passover is sacrificed for us: Therefore let us keep the feast, not with old leaven, neither with the leaven of malice and wickedness; but with the unleavened bread of sincerity and truth. (1 Corinthians 5:6-8)

FELLOWSHIP ATTAINED BY THE SHARING OF THE HOST WITH A DEVOTED, INVOLVED PASTOR

> And upon the first day of the week, when the disciples came together to break bread, Paul preached unto them, ready to depart on the morrow; and continued his speech until midnight. (Acts 20:7)

Jesus brings truth and gives eternal life for the eater of the bread. All penitent, obedient, well-confessed sinners must receive the Host, including the priest, the congregants, and all who come with the hope of seeing Eternal Life.

> Verily, verily, I say unto you, He that believeth on me hath everlasting life. I am that bread of life. Your fathers did eat manna in the wilderness, and are dead. This is the bread which cometh down from Heaven, that a man may eat thereof, and not die. I am the living bread which came down from heaven: if any man eat of this bread, he shall live for ever: and the bread that I will give is my

APPENDIX A: The Bible Is the True Source of the Traditional Anglican Mass - A Biblical Sacramental Reference Guide

flesh, which I will give for the life of the world. The Jews therefore strove among themselves, saying, How can this Man give us His flesh to eat? Then Jesus said unto them, Verily, verily, I say unto you, Except ye eat the flesh of the Son of man, and drink His blood, ye have no life in you. Whoso eateth my flesh, and drinketh my blood, hath eternal life; and I will raise him up at the last day. For my flesh is meat indeed, and my blood is drink indeed. He that eateth my flesh, and drinketh my blood, dwelleth in me, and I in him. As the living Father hath sent me, and I live by the Father: so he that eateth me, even he shall live by me. This is that bread which came down from heaven: not as your fathers did eat manna, and are dead: he that eateth of this bread shall live for ever. (John 6:47-58)

And did all drink the same spiritual drink: for they drank of that spiritual Rock that followed them: and that Rock was Christ. (1 Corinthians 10:4)

And they, continuing daily with one accord in the temple, and breaking bread from house to house, did eat their meat with gladness and singleness of heart. (Acts 2:46)

APPENDIX A: *The Bible Is the True Source of the Traditional Anglican Mass – A Biblical Sacramental Reference Guide*

JESUS IS THE REAL PRESIDER OVER THE LITURGY: CHRIST THE PROPHET, PRIEST, AND KING

> And Jesus came and spake unto them, saying, All power is given unto me in heaven and in earth. (Matthew 28:18)

> And it came to pass, as He sat at meat with them, he took bread, and blessed it, and brake, and gave to them. (Luke 24:30)

> Wherefore God also hath highly exalted Him, and given Him a name which is above every name: That at the name of Jesus every knee should bow, of things in heaven, and things in earth, and things under the earth; And that every tongue should confess that Jesus Christ is Lord, to the glory of God the Father. (Philippians 2:9-11)

> And He is the head of the body, the church: who is the beginning, the firstborn from the dead; that in all things he might have the preeminence. (Colossians 1:18)

> Far above all principality and power, and might, and dominion, and every name that is named, not only in this world, but also in that which is to come: And hath put all things under His feet, and gave Him to be the head over all things to the church which is His body, the fulness of Him that filleth all in all. (Ephesians 1:21-23)

APPENDIX A: The Bible Is the True Source of the Traditional Anglican Mass – A Biblical Sacramental Reference Guide

DAVID WAS NOT LYING WHEN HE SAID HE WAS ON A MISSION FOR "THE KING"

> Then came David to Nob to Ahimelech the priest: and Ahimelech was afraid at the meeting of David, and said unto him, Why art thou alone, and no man with thee? And David said unto Ahimelech the priest, The king hath commanded me a business, and hath said unto me, Let no man know any thing of the business whereabout I send thee, and what I have commanded thee: and I have appointed my servants to such and such a place. Now therefore what is under thine hand? give me five loaves of bread in mine hand, or what there is present. And the priest answered David, and said, There is no common bread under mine hand, but there is hallowed bread; if the young men have kept themselves at least from women. And David answered the priest, and said unto him, Of a truth women have been kept from us about these three days, since I came out, and the vessels of the young men are holy, and the bread is in a manner common, yea, though it were sanctified this day in the vessel. So the priest gave him hallowed bread: for there was no bread there but the shewbread, that was taken from before the Lord, to put hot bread in the day when it was taken away. (1 Samuel 21:1-6)

It was never actually King Saul, but Christ indeed. Now, by pretextual extension, it was also David, the anointed shepherd, who in fear of King

APPENDIX A: The Bible Is the True Source of the Traditional Anglican Mass - A Biblical Sacramental Reference Guide

Saul, took it on the lam. He spoke the Truth of Logos, rather than spewing a falsehood when he stopped in Nob. He needed eat the holy bread to survive Saul's chase, so that he and his men could end up surviving in order to sit on the throne of Judah. This eternal invisible seat would eventually situate David's descendent, Christ the King and Savior, the Lion of this Tribe of Judah. David's comrades, described as pure and perhaps even celibate, are the placeholders for the 24 Elders who will stand in the throne room of God, a priesthood in Heaven (Revelation 4:4).

WHY THE MIRACLE OF THE REAL PRESENCE HAPPENS BY GOD'S WILL, NOT BY THAT OF THE CHURCH OR HER PRIESTS

> And it came to pass, that He went through the corn fields on the sabbath day; and His disciples began, as they went, to pluck the ears of corn. And the Pharisees said unto him, Behold, why do they on the Sabbath day that which is not lawful? And He said unto them, Have ye never read what David did, when he had need, and was an hungred, he, and they that were with him? How he went into the house of God in the days of Abiathar the high priest, and did eat the shewbread, which is not lawful to eat but for the priests, and gave also to them which were with him? And He said unto them, The Sabbath was made for man, and not man for the Sabbath: Therefore the Son of man is Lord also of the Sabbath. (Mark 2:23-28)

APPENDIX A: The Bible Is the True Source of the Traditional Anglican Mass – A Biblical Sacramental Reference Guide

Weekly Holy Communion must happen during hours between the lunar ascendence of Saturday evening as it commences Vespers, and on any of the hours of the Sunday that continue that Christian Sabbath. Just as the Father had given the shewbread of Ahimelech to David, humanity has been bequeathed the Sabbath, a gift by which the miracle of the Eucharist will fulfill Christians.

> Thus the heavens and the earth were finished, and all the host of them. And on the seventh day God ended His work which He had made; and He rested on the seventh day from all His work which He had made. (Genesis 2:1-3)

> The sabbath was made for man, and not man for the sabbath: therefore the Son of man is Lord also of the sabbath. (Mark 2:27-28)

The Sabbath was thus given by Jesus to man to enjoy. The Christian sanctuary, where the Eucharist is prepared, projects both the image of its Mosaic origin and God's will. Regardless of whether the Sabbath is Saturday or has been moved from Saturday to Sunday, God, as the Lord of the Sabbath, is above the Sabbath and He has made the Sabbath for man.

> And other of their brethren, of the sons of the Kohathites, were over the shewbread, to prepare it every Sabbath. (1 Chronicles 9:32)

> And their charge shall be the ark, and the table, and the candlestick, and the altars, and

APPENDIX A: The Bible Is the True Source of the Traditional
Anglican Mass - A Biblical Sacramental Reference Guide

> the vessels of the sanctuary wherewith they minister, and the hanging, and all the service thereof. And Eleazar the son of Aaron the priest shall be chief over the chief of the Levites, and have the oversight of them that keep the charge of the sanctuary. (Numbers 3:31-32)

The priest, his sacristan or sexton, and his altar servers store, count, and ready the Bread and Wine for Holy Communion just as the descendants of Kohath (the son of Levi), were charged with caring for and protecting the Ark of the Covenant, the Menorah, and the Table of Shewbread.

THE DECALOGUE UPLIFTS THE SIGNIFICANCE OF THE LAW THROUGHOUT THE MASS

> But he who was of the bondwoman was born after the flesh; but he of the freewoman was by promise. Which things are an allegory: for these are the two covenants; the one from the mount Sinai, which gendereth to bondage, which is Agar. For this Agar is mount Sinai in Arabia, and answereth to Jerusalem which now is, and is in bondage with her children. But Jerusalem which is above is free, which is the mother of us all. (Galatians 4:23-26)

As theoria *is the gazing upon the Liturgy for spiritual enrichment, so then is consumption of the consecrated Eucharist proof of how Christ has abrogated the death of the sinner from any stipulation owed to the Covenant of the Law of*

APPENDIX A: The Bible Is the True Source of the Traditional Anglican Mass - A Biblical Sacramental Reference Guide

Moses. Holy Communion moves the Christian inside the brand-new, joyful context of the New Covenant of Christ's Grace, whereby the sinner with graceful Faith shall be saved. Saint Paul of Tarsus gives his allegory of Hagar and Sarah, the two women who bore children to Abraham to teach this. Hagar illustrates the Covenant of the Law, but Sarah illustrates the eternal promise of the Covenant of Grace.

> For I through the law am dead to the law, that I might live unto God. (Galatians 2:19)

> For as many as are of the works of the law are under the curse: for it is written, Cursed is every one that continueth not in all things which are written in the book of the law to do them. But that no man is justified by the law in the sight of God, it is evident: for, The just shall live by faith. And the law is not of faith: but, the man that doeth them shall live in them. Christ hath redeemed us from the curse of the law, being made a curse for us: for it is written, Cursed is every one that hangeth on a tree. (Galatians 10:3-1)

> They clave to their brethren, their nobles, and entered into a curse, and into an oath, to walk in God's law, which was given by Moses the servant of God, and to observe and do all the commandments of the Lord our Lord, and his judgments and his statutes. (Nehemiah 10:29)

APPENDIX A: The Bible Is the True Source of the Traditional Anglican Mass - A Biblical Sacramental Reference Guide

Man, without seeking Salvation through Christ, has only the illumination of his intellect and flawed Free Will to guide his attempt to live by the Law. Although the Law had enabled the Hebrews to survive 40 years in the wilderness, it did not prevent the destruction of Israel. The builders of the Wall of the Second Temple clearly realized that Israel had for 800 years been living, not according to love of God, but according to their fear of invoking the curse penalizing them for breaking the law.

> For I am persuaded, that neither death, nor life, nor angels, nor principalities, nor powers, nor things present, nor things to come, nor height, nor depth, nor any other creature, shall be able to separate us from the love of God, which is in Christ Jesus our Lord. (Romans 8:38-39)

Christ busted this curse, which no man, without the Salvation solely possible through Jesus, can avoid damnably incurring to himself. Thus, people must live by the love of God, not according to fear of destruction. "There is no fear in love; but perfect love casteth out fear: because fear hath torment. He that feareth is not made perfect in love" (1 John 4:18).

APPROACH THE COMMUNION TABLE OBEDIENTLY AND IN UPRIGHT FELLOWSHIP

> "For the precious death and merits of thy Son Jesus Christ our Lord, and for the sending to us of the Holy Ghost, the Comforter; who are

APPENDIX A: The Bible Is the True Source of the Traditional Anglican Mass – A Biblical Sacramental Reference Guide

one with thee in thy Eternal Godhead" (Preface; *1928 Book of Common Prayer*).

The Preface for Trinity Sunday *reminds us of our rebirth as the "lump" of the "First Fruit" (Romans 11:16). That is, our Salvation, Christ Jesus, has been prepared for us by the Father, together with His counterpart, the Holy Ghost, in the three-way* perichoresis. *The Holy Ghost, also known as the Comforter, is always ministering to us in order to keep us focused and untroubled. "And I will pray the Father, and he shall give you another Comforter, that he may abide with you forever; even the Spirit of truth" (John 14:16-17a).*

For verily I say unto you, Till heaven and earth pass, one jot or one tittle shall in no wise pass from the law, till all be fulfilled. (Matthew 5:18)

Neither do I condemn thee: go, and sin no more. (John 8:11)

While the Law may signify death for the unrepentant sinner, the Law is itself fully alive— as Jesus. He will separate the sheep from the goats (Matthew 25:32-46).

BEWARE OF THE PRIDE AND VAINGLORY THAT JADE AND DIVIDE A CONGREGATION

For if the casting away of them be the reconciling of the world, what shall the receiving of them be, but life from the dead? For if the firstfruit be holy, the lump is also

APPENDIX A: The Bible Is the True Source of the Traditional Anglican Mass - A Biblical Sacramental Reference Guide

holy: and if the root be holy, so are the branches. And if some of the branches be broken off, and thou, being a wild olive tree, wert grafted in among them, and with them partakest of the root and fatness of the olive tree; Boast not against the branches. But if thou boast, thou bearest not the root, but the root thee. Thou wilt say then, The branches were broken off, that I might be grafted in. Well; because of unbelief they were broken off, and thou standest by faith. Be not highminded, but fear: For if God spared not the natural branches, take heed lest he also spare not thee. Behold therefore the goodness and severity of God: on them which fell, severity; but toward thee, goodness, if thou continue in his goodness: otherwise thou also shalt be cut off. And they also, if they abide not still in unbelief, shall be grafted in: for God is able to graft them in again. For if thou wert cut out of the olive tree which is wild by nature, and wert grafted contrary to nature into a good olive tree: how much more shall these, which be the natural branches, be grafted into their own olive tree? (Romans 11:15-24)

Sometimes called "spiritual gluttony," the boasting and competitiveness between congregants is known to be accompanied by claiming pew spaces; dressing immodestly; flaunting wealth to cause privilege and favoritism; the forming of cliques, variance, and faction (Galatians 5:20). The Law is alive in Jesus, who will judge such disobedience fittingly, and

APPENDIX A: *The Bible Is the True Source of the Traditional Anglican Mass - A Biblical Sacramental Reference Guide*

prune away the sinful branches until the Church Triumphant contains only the "good lump." Moreover, although the pharisaical Jews and Gentile children of disobedience have been cut off, there is still time during anyone's life nevertheless to reconcile to God.

THE THREE CREEDS

> Hear, O Israel: The Lord our God is one Lord: And thou shalt love the Lord thy God with all thine heart, and with all thy soul, and with all thy might. And these words, which I command thee this day, shall be in thine heart: And thou shalt teach them diligently unto thy children, and shalt talk of them when thou sittest in thine house, and when thou walkest by the way, and when thou liest down, and when thou risest up. And thou shalt bind them for a sign upon thine hand, and they shall be as frontlets between thine eyes. And thou shalt write them upon the posts of thy house, and on thy gates. (Deuteronomy 6:4-9)

> One God and Father of all, who is above all, and through all, and in you all. (Ephesians 4:6)

Only the Love of God can save us. The metaphysics of Christ's nature and Love must be reviewed every week via the Apostle's Creed *or the* Nicene Creed *(and, on certain occasions, the long-form* Athanasian Creed*). Much like the Jews profess of the oneness of God by affixing*

APPENDIX A: The Bible Is the True Source of the Traditional Anglican Mass – A Biblical Sacramental Reference Guide

mezuzahs on their doorways and walls, Christians around the world recite the Nicene Creed as a profession that firmly roots the faithful in the orthodoxy and catholicity (and hence unity) of traditional Christendom.

WHO PROCEEDS FROM THE FATHER AND THE SON (*FILIOQUE*)

> But when the Comforter is come, Whom I will send unto you from the Father, even the Spirit of truth, which proceedeth from the Father, He shall testify of Me. (John 15:26)

The clause in the Creeds known as the Filioque, *which literally means "and the Son," is an ontological reference to the Omnipresence of the Son, Who, with the Father, sends the Holy Spirit to people. Although the Great Schism that separated the Eastern and Western Churches (A.D. 1054) was partially caused when the Byzantine patriarchs insisted that only the Father sends the Comforter, Christ Jesus indeed collaborates with God, but always doing nothing without His Father's authority (John 5:30), given permission to partake in this dispatching of the Holy Ghost to humankind, according to John 15. It should also not be forgotten that five chapters later in the book of John, Jesus "breathed" on the Apostles, directly imparting unto them the Holy Ghost (John 20:21-23). And so the Filioque remains rooted in the Faith Tradition of the Anglican Church and the rest of the Western Churches as a fully legitimate expression of the Christian Faith.*

APPENDIX A: The Bible Is the True Source of the Traditional Anglican Mass - A Biblical Sacramental Reference Guide

> But the scripture hath concluded all under sin, that the promise by faith of Jesus Christ might be given to them that believe. But before faith came, we were kept under the law, shut up unto the faith which should afterwards be revealed. Wherefore the law was our schoolmaster to bring us unto Christ, that we might be justified by faith. But after that faith is come, we are no longer under a schoolmaster. For ye are all the children of God by faith in Christ Jesus. (Galatians 3:22-26)

As the brethren come together in Fellowship with Christ, it becomes more discernible that a people in a state of Grace know that both the New Covenant of Grace and the Old Covenant of the Law of Moses have grown together in great relevance to the ecclesiastical Faith that already binds them in Holy Communion.

THE "OUR FATHER" IS RECITED BY A HUMBLE CHURCH IN CATHOLIC UNITY

> Woe unto you that are full! for ye shall hunger. Woe unto you that laugh now! for ye shall mourn and weep. (Luke 6:25)

> And He said, Therefore said I unto you, that no man can come unto Me, except it were given unto him of My Father. (John 6:65)

Sinners thirst to be carried to the Kingdom of God by following Christ alone. Those with puffed-up arrogance are led into all sorts of temptations.

APPENDIX A: The Bible Is the True Source of the Traditional Anglican Mass - A Biblical Sacramental Reference Guide

But the church asks to be delivered from evils such as the gnostic whisperings of "New Thought" and "Laws of Attraction."

THE REAL PRESENCE IN THE BREAD AND WINE

> The cup of blessing which we bless, is it not the communion of the blood of Christ? The bread which we break, is it not the communion of the body of Christ? For we being many are one bread, and one body: for we are all partakers of that one bread. Behold Israel after the flesh: are not they which eat of the sacrifices partakers of the altar?
> (1 Corinthians 10:16-18)

The priest, during the epiclesis *(i.e., the Invocation of the Holy Spirit), beseeches God to transform the bread and wine into the Body and Blood of Christ. The Communicant consumes the Eucharist and thus says, "Amen."*

THE PRAYER OF HUMBLE ACCESS

> And when he had taken the five loaves and the two fishes, he looked up to heaven, and blessed, and brake the loaves, and gave them to his disciples to set before them; and the two fishes divided he among them all.
> (Mark 6:41)

> And the Spirit and the bride say, Come. And let him that heareth say, Come. And let him that is athirst come. And whosoever will, let

APPENDIX A: The Bible Is the True Source of the Traditional Anglican Mass - A Biblical Sacramental Reference Guide

> him take the water of life freely. (Revelation 22:17)

> Truly I tell you, unless you change and become like little children, you will never enter the Kingdom of Heaven. Therefore, whoever takes the lowly position of this child is the greatest in the kingdom of Heaven. (Matthew 18:2-4)

Coming to the table with a pure heart requires Faith—that is, the assurance and conviction of things hoped for yet not seen (2 Corinthians 4:18).

THE COMFORTABLE WORDS

> Come unto me, all ye that labour and are heavy laden, and I will give you rest. (Matthew 11:28)

These are verses contemplating the Absolution and Remission of Sin, whereby the Confessor had given the Invitation: "Draw near with Faith."

WEEKLY HOLY COMMUNION: THE PROPITIATION FOR OUR SIN—CHRIST, WHO IS THE END OF THE LAW

> For He hath made Him to be sin for us, Who knew no sin; that we might be made the righteousness of God in Him. (2 Corinthians 5:21)

APPENDIX A: The Bible Is the True Source of the Traditional Anglican Mass - A Biblical Sacramental Reference Guide

> Let us draw near with a true heart in full assurance of faith, having our hearts sprinkled from an evil conscience, and our bodies washed with pure water. Let us hold fast the profession of our Faith without wavering; (for He is faithful that promised). And let us consider one another to provoke unto love and to good works: Not forsaking the assembling of ourselves together, as the manner of some is; but exhorting one another: and so much the more, as ye see the day approaching. (Hebrews 10:22-25)

Retaining the solemnity of the Law of Moses found in Exodus 20 and Deuteronomy 5, human obedience is still pledged to follow the Law but to do so by following Christ, Who is the fulfillment of the Law of the Old Covenant through the New Covenant of Grace, Christ Jesus showing forth the Love of God, Who alone redeems us.

> Thou shalt love the Lord thy God with all thy heart, and with all thy soul, and with all thy mind. This being the first and great commandment. And the second is like unto it; Thou shalt love thy neighbor as thyself. On these two commandments hang all the Law and the Prophets. (Matthew 22:37-40)

Although the Traditional-Anglican Liturgy (i.e., the 1928 BCP) eases dietary and collateral restrictions with its Table of Fasts and Feasts, God is asked to cleanse the heart during Confession. Moreover, the rubrics of the Decalogue hold that each communicant "shall, after every

APPENDIX A: The Bible Is the True Source of the Traditional Anglican Mass – A Biblical Sacramental Reference Guide

Commandment, ask God mercy for their transgressions for the time past, and Grace to keep the law for the time to come," making reference to the "First and Second Great Commandments," as our Savior taught us.

> And this day shall be unto you for a memorial; and ye shall keep it a feast to the Lord throughout your generations; ye shall keep it a feast by an ordinance forever. Seven days shall ye eat unleavened bread; even the first day ye shall put away leaven out of your houses: for whosoever eateth leavened bread from the first day until the seventh day, that soul shall be cut off from Israel. And in the first day there shall be an holy convocation, and in the seventh day there shall be an holy convocation to you; no manner of work shall be done in them, save that which every man must eat, that only may be done of you. And ye shall observe the feast of unleavened bread; for in this selfsame day have I brought your armies out of the land of Egypt: therefore shall ye observe this day in your generations by an ordinance for ever. (Exodus 12:14-17)

The Ordinal of Holy Communion was given in its original stricter form by the Father through the Law of Moses, even though God had, as explicated by Christ (Mark 2:23-28), made the Sabbath day for man, and not man for the Sabbath.

APPENDIX A: The Bible Is the True Source of the Traditional Anglican Mass - A Biblical Sacramental Reference Guide

INDWELLING VIA THE EUCHARIST

> And when the children of Israel saw it, they said one to another, It is manna: for they wist not what it was. And Moses said unto them, This is the bread which the Lord hath given you to eat. (Exodus 16:15).

> And here we offer and present unto thee, O Lord, our selves, our souls and bodies, to be a reasonable, holy, and living sacrifice unto thee; humbly beseeching thee, that we, and all others who shall be partakers of this Holy Communion, may worthily receive the most precious Body and Blood of thy Son Jesus Christ, be filled with thy grace and heavenly benediction, and made one body with Him, that He may dwell in us, and we in Him. (Oblation/Invocation; 1928 *Book of Common Prayer*)

During Holy Communion, communicants are indeed "beseeching" God for the true Bread of Heaven, who is Christ. The 1928 BCP calls to mind that it is God's choice, not the theologian's decision, or the priest's doing, as to what invisible occurrence, transformation, or conversion, takes place during the epiclesis. The bread of Fellowship, after all, fell from Heaven every day for the Hebrews of the Exodus.

The words of the well-confessed Communicant humbly reading from the 1928 BCP are clearly voicings of imploration of God that a mystical incarnation will indeed happen, every Sunday,

APPENDIX A: The Bible Is the True Source of the Traditional Anglican Mass – A Biblical Sacramental Reference Guide

until they can join in ultimate theosis *with God, that is, the Fellowship of the oneness with God for all eternity. They are, after all, intending to receive the pouring out of the Holy Spirit, sharing themselves with the Eucharist as the "kindling" of oblation.*

> And it shall come to pass afterward, that I will pour out my spirit upon all flesh; and your sons and your daughters shall prophesy, your old men shall dream dreams, your young men shall see visions. (Joel 2:28)

> For I will pour water upon him that is thirsty, and floods upon the dry ground: I will pour my spirit upon thy seed, and my blessing upon thine offspring. (Isaiah 44:3)

> And it shall come to pass in the last days, saith God, I will pour out of my Spirit upon all flesh: and your sons and your daughters shall prophesy, and your young men shall see visions, and your old men shall dream dreams. (Acts 2:17)

> And they came to the place which God had told him of; and Abraham built an altar there, and laid the wood in order, and bound Isaac his son, and laid him on the altar upon the wood. And Abraham stretched forth his hand, and took the knife to slay his son. And the angel of the Lord called unto him out of Heaven, and said, Abraham, Abraham: and he said, Here am I ... And said, By myself have I sworn, saith the Lord, for because thou hast

APPENDIX A: The Bible Is the True Source of the Traditional Anglican Mass – A Biblical Sacramental Reference Guide

done this thing, and hast not withheld thy son, thine only son: That in blessing I will bless thee, and in multiplying I will multiply thy seed as the stars of the heaven, and as the sand which is upon the sea shore; and thy seed shall possess the gate of his enemies. And in thy seed shall all the nations of the earth be blessed; because thou hast obeyed my voice. (Genesis 22: 9-11, 16-18)

CHRIST IS THE TRUE CONSECRATOR OF THE BREAD AND WINE

And He commanded the multitude to sit down on the grass, and took the five loaves, and the two fishes, and looking up to heaven, he blessed, and brake, and gave the loaves to his disciples, and the disciples to the multitude. (Matthew 14:19)

And as they were eating, Jesus took bread, and blessed it, and brake it, and gave it to the disciples, and said, Take, eat; this is my body. (Matthew 26:26)

In this book, we have concentrated on ancient but profound terms such as theoria *and* perichoresis *to help describe the way that God brings Christians together to focus upon the mystery of His Grace-filled works in church. Churches do not need gimmicks, raffles, bake sales, and entertainment to hold people in reverence—if anything, these things can tend toward producing the opposite result. The Bible shows that Christ did not need anything more than our observant*

APPENDIX A: *The Bible Is the True Source of the Traditional Anglican Mass – A Biblical Sacramental Reference Guide*

Faith and obedience to feed the multitude with His Grace.

> The Lord is my Shepherd; I shall not want. He maketh me to lie down in green pastures: He leadeth me beside the still waters. He restoreth my soul: He leadeth me in the paths of righteousness for His name's sake. Yea, though I walk through the valley of the shadow of death, I will fear no evil: for thou art with me; thy rod and thy staff they comfort me. Thou preparest a table before me in the presence of mine enemies: Thou anointest my head with oil; my cup runneth over. Surely goodness and mercy shall follow me all the days of my life: and I will dwell in the house of the Lord for ever. (Psalm 23)
>
> I will not leave you comfortless: I will come to you. Yet a little while, and the world seeth me no more; but ye see me: because I live, ye shall live also. (John 14:19-20)

The promise of Fellowship with God has been the Father's promise since time began, just as Christ has promised to make Himself present again in every Eucharist.

A FAITHFUL, HUMBLE PRIEST MUST INVOKE CHRIST TO ARREST THE FALLING AWAY OF THE FAITHFUL

> Moreover, He said unto me, Son of man, eat that thou findest; eat this roll, and go speak unto the house of Israel. So I opened my

mouth, and He caused me to eat that roll. And He said unto me, Son of man, cause thy belly to eat, and fill thy bowels with this roll that I give thee. Then did I eat it; and it was in my mouth as honey for sweetness. And He said unto me, Son of man, go, get thee unto the house of Israel, and speak with My Words unto them. (Ezekiel 3:1-4)

Just as a third of the angels rebelled along with Satan (Revelation 12:4), Christendom will experience a "falling away" to buy Lucifer's deceits (2 Thessalonians 2:3), with about two-thirds lost, leaving only about one-third as a remnant. Ezekiel 5:4-5 calls this very fraction to mind when Israel is surrounded by enemy nations and scorched and maimed during the Apocalypse. And in Zechariah 13:8, we see the same theme: "And it shall come to pass, that in all the land, saith the Lord, two parts therein shall be cut off and die; but the third shall be left therein." The priesthood therefore must consume the Word of God with both the example of his upright life and the consumption of the Body and Blood so that more souls can be delivered from this Great Apostasy that has been foretold.

THANKSGIVING: "THY KINGDOM COME, THY WILL BE DONE, ON EARTH AS IT IS IN HEAVEN"

Almighty and everliving God, we most heartily thank thee, for that thou dost vouchsafe to feed us who have duly received these holy mysteries with the spiritual food of the most precious Body and Blood of thy

APPENDIX A: The Bible Is the True Source of the Traditional Anglican Mass - A Biblical Sacramental Reference Guide

> Son our Saviour Jesus Christ; and dost assure us thereby of thy favour and goodness towards us; and that we are very members incorporate in the mystical body of thy Son, which is the blessed company of all faithful people; and are also heirs through hope of thy everlasting kingdom, by the merits of his most precious death and passion. (Thanksgiving; *1928 Book of Common Prayer*)

The 1928 BCP leads us in giving thanks to Almighty God, after the Eucharist is consumed, that the human soul has been enjoined with the most precious Body and Blood of Christ.

> No man can come to me, except the Father which hath sent me draw Him: and I will raise Him up at the last day. It is written in the prophets, And they shall be all taught of God. Every man therefore that hath heard, and hath learned of the Father, cometh unto Me. (John 6:44-45)

> Behold, I shew you a mystery; we shall not all sleep, but we shall all be changed, in a moment, in the twinkling of an eye, at the last trump: for the trumpet shall sound, and the dead shall be raised incorruptible, and we shall be changed. (1 Corinthians 15)

Thus the eucharistic act of Grace continues the Sacramental preparation that was begun at our Baptisms, to advance toward the Resurrection of our risen, glorified bodies; the Rapture; to our

APPENDIX A: The Bible Is the True Source of the Traditional Anglican Mass – A Biblical Sacramental Reference Guide

Redemption—all conducted by the Son, enacting the Father's authority.

WHY ARE CHRISTIANS INVITED TO MASS TO ENJOY THE LITURGY AND RECEIVE HOLY COMMUNION?

> Ho, every one that thirsteth, come ye to the waters, and he that hath no money; come ye, buy, and eat; yea, come, buy wine and milk without money and without price. Wherefore do ye spend money for that which is not bread? and your labour for that which satisfieth not? hearken diligently unto me, and eat ye that which is good, and let your soul delight itself in fatness. Incline your ear, and come unto me: hear, and your soul shall live; and I will make an everlasting covenant with you, even the sure mercies of David. (Isaiah 55:1-3)

> Come unto me, all he that labor and are heavy laden, and I will give you rest. Take my yoke upon you, and learn of me; for I am meek and lowly in heart: and ye shall find rust unto your souls. (Matthew 11:28-29)

It is useful to ask, how do we know that God wants us to get together at Church? What biblical origin exists for the calling forth of the Faithful to weekly Mass? Was there a charitable invitation issued in Scripture that Christians should consider? It is fitting for the mind to hearken back to this holy outreach, seeing these verses as the beautiful pretext for the great ancient

APPENDIX A: The Bible Is the True Source of the Traditional Anglican Mass - A Biblical Sacramental Reference Guide

liturgies that followed. Let us remind ourselves how the Bible orients this great Fellowship to commence even today, with its loving exchange between the Priest and Congregation, "The Lord be with you/And with thy spirit" and "Let us pray" and all that follows.

Thus, the biblical basis for the attainment of communion with Christ and one another during the Mass is well portrayed by the prophet Isaiah, who made it clear that Truth nourishes the heart of every listener as the priceless free reward shared between equals for their Faith and participation, as if celebrating at a great feast. Moreover, the invitation to "come unto me" is reiterated by Our Lord in Matthew 11.

THE REVELATION THAT OPENS THE MASS AND CADENCES THE *EPICLESIS*

> After this manner therefore pray ye: Our Father which art in Heaven, Hallowed be Thy Name. Thy kingdom come, Thy will be done in earth, as it is in Heaven. Give us this day our daily bread. And forgive us our debts, as we forgive our debtors. And lead us not into temptation, but deliver us from evil: For thine is the kingdom, and the power, and the glory, for ever. Amen. (Matthew 6:9-13)

THE SECOND COMING (*PAROUSIA*) IN THE NICENE CREED, ALTAR FACING EAST

> And His feet shall stand in that day upon the mount of Olives, which is before Jerusalem

APPENDIX A: The Bible Is the True Source of the Traditional Anglican Mass - A Biblical Sacramental Reference Guide

on the east, and the mount of Olives shall cleave in the midst thereof toward the east and toward the west, and there shall be a very great valley; and half of the mountain shall remove toward the north, and half of it toward the south. (Zechariah 14:4)

But who may abide the day of his coming? And who shall stand when he appeareth? For he is like a refiner's fire, and like fuller's soap: And he shall sit as refiner and purifier of silver: and he shall purify the sons of Levi, and purge them as gold and silver, that they may offer unto the Lord and offering in righteousness. (Malachi 3:2-3)

Behold, he cometh with clouds; and every eye shall see Him, and they also which pierced Him: and all kindreds of the earth shall wail because of Him. Even so, Amen. (Revelation 1:7)

So Christ was once offered to bear the sins of many; and unto them that look for Him shall He appear the second time without sin unto salvation. (Hebrews 9:28)

During the Apocalypse, the persecuted Church Militant will be surrounded on all sides, but Christ (Logos) will vanquish Satan from Eternal Memory (Revelation 22).

In my Father's house are many mansions: if it were not so, I would have told you. And if I go and prepare a place for you, I will come

APPENDIX A: The Bible Is the True Source of the Traditional
Anglican Mass - A Biblical Sacramental Reference Guide

> again, and receive you unto Myself; that
> where I am, there ye may be also. (John 14:3)
>
> When Christ, Who is our life, shall appear,
> then shall ye also appear with Him in glory.
> (Colossians 3:4)
>
> Beloved, now are we the sons of God, and it
> doth now yet appear what we shall be: but we
> know that, when He shall appear, we shall be
> like Him; for we shall see Him as He is.
> (1 John 3:2)

*The Lord will lead us to His Home, which is
Heaven, and we shall become like Him there.*

THE METAPHYSICS OF JESUS, WHO IS GOD, THE CHRIST, WHO IS THE ETERNAL WORD

> In the beginning was the Word, and the Word
> was with God, and the Word was God. The
> same was in the beginning with God. All
> things were made by him; and without him
> was not any thing made that was made. In
> Him was life; and the life was the light of
> men. And the light shineth in darkness; and
> the darkness comprehended it not. There was
> a man sent from God, whose name was John.
> The same came for a witness, to bear witness
> of the Light, that all men through him might
> believe. He was not that Light, but was sent
> to bear witness of that Light. That was the
> true Light, which lighteth every man that
> cometh into the world. He was in the world,
> and the world was made by Him, and the

APPENDIX A: The Bible Is the True Source of the Traditional Anglican Mass - A Biblical Sacramental Reference Guide

world knew Him not. He came unto his own, and His own received him not. But as many as received Him, to them gave He power to become the sons of God, even to them that believe on his name: Which were born, not of blood, nor of the will of the flesh, nor of the will of man, but of God. And the Word was made flesh, and dwelt among us, (and we beheld His glory, the glory as of the only begotten of the Father,) full of grace and truth. John [the Baptist] bare witness of Him, and cried, saying, This was He of whom I spake, He that cometh after me is preferred before me: for He was before me. And of His fulness have all we received, and grace for grace. For the law was given by Moses, but grace and truth came by Jesus Christ. No man hath seen God at any time, the only begotten Son, which is in the bosom of the Father, He hath declared Him. (John 1:1-18)

It could rightfully be said that the entire Bible is written in the first chapter of the Gospel of Saint John. The Ontological Independence of the Father, upon Whom all things depend for their existence, is the Creator of everything out of nothingness (Genesis 1). John the Visionary predicates God's existence in terms of the twofold purpose of His existence: God's Metaphysics, in that He created everything and exists in that He exists (Exodus 3:14) and thus inspired all the prophets and their words (i.e., in the Ketuvim, the Tanakh, and the Nevi'im of the Torah); and his Perfect Love, in that He so loved the world that He gave us His only Son (Who is also God) so that by

APPENDIX A: The Bible Is the True Source of the Traditional Anglican Mass – A Biblical Sacramental Reference Guide

His death we might be saved from the Second Death (John 3:16; Revelation 20:14). It can therefore be known that God's Word is the unfailing credibility of the perfect Love by which He both created and, via His Son, intends to save us. All Systematic Theology stems from this moral theology and metaphysics, sketched beautifully as the "more-real" version of Genesis, that is, in the First Chapter of the Gospel of John.

THE WORD THAT BUTTRESSES THE LITURGY IS ETERNAL

> Verily I say unto you, This generation shall not pass, till all these things be fulfilled. Heaven and earth shall pass away, but My Words shall not pass away. (Matthew 24:34-35; Mark 13:30-31; Luke 21:32-33)

DOXOLOGY

> And every creature which is in Heaven, and on the earth, and under the earth, and such as are in the sea, and all that are in them, heard I saying, Blessing, and honour, and glory, and power, be unto Him that sitteth upon the throne, and unto the Lamb forever and ever. (Revelation 5:13)

The word "Doxology" comes from the Greek word for thanksgiving, doxologia (Δοξολογία). From the many verses giving God praise in the Bible, the lyricist Thomas Ken penned in 1709, "Praise God from Whom All Blessings Flow" (The Hymnal of the Protestant Episcopal Church in the United

APPENDIX A: The Bible Is the True Source of the Traditional Anglican Mass - A Biblical Sacramental Reference Guide

States of America; Hymn 139; 1940). The Doxology signifies that all creatures with their vitality and/or words instantiate gratitude to the Creator, Who redeems the sins of His people and asks man to emulate Him. In fact, even should no creature be able to praise Almighty God, even the very stones would immediately cry out (Luke 19:37-40).

> That the trial of your faith, being much more precious than of gold that perisheth, though it be tried with fire, might be found unto praise and honour and glory at the appearing of Jesus Christ. (1 Peter 1:7)

> Learn to do well; seek judgment, relieve the oppressed, judge the fatherless, plead for the widow. Come now, and let us reason together, saith the Lord: though your sins be as scarlet, they shall be as white as snow; though they be red like crimson, they shall be as wool. If ye be willing and obedient, ye shall eat the good of the land. (Isaiah 1:17-19)

It is at the time of the recitation of the Doxology, during which we praise God for all of creation, that the priest pours the wine and water into the same chalice, while the tithes are brought to the altar by the altar server. The priest meanwhile prayerfully exhorts generosity for the needy.

APPENDIX A: The Bible Is the True Source of the Traditional Anglican Mass - A Biblical Sacramental Reference Guide

THE PROMISE THAT HOLY COMMUNION EXPONENTIATES GRACE IN CHURCHES

> In the last day, that great day of the feast, Jesus stood and cried, saying, If any man thirst, let him come unto me, and drink. He that believeth on me as the scripture hath said, out of his belly shall flow rivers of living water. (John 7:37-38)

The Eucharistic Liturgy does not happen in a vacuum. When it is executed by a faithful Congregation and Priest, Grace is poured out and multiplied, spread by word of mouth and the proliferation of good deeds, and hence the church grows and flourishes.

GOOD TRINITARIAN CHRISTIANS WHO "INTEND TO LEAD A NEW LIFE" MAY RECEIVE TRADITIONAL ANGLICAN COMMUNION

> In my Father's house are many mansions: if it were not so, I would have told you. I go to prepare a place for you. (John 14:2)

> Ye who do truly and earnestly repent you of your sins, and are in love and charity with your neighbours, and intend to lead a new life, following the commandments of God, and walking from henceforth in his holy ways; Draw near with faith, and take this holy Sacrament to your comfort; and make your humble confession to Almighty God, devoutly kneeling. (*1928 Book of Common Prayer*)

APPENDIX A: *The Bible Is the True Source of the Traditional Anglican Mass - A Biblical Sacramental Reference Guide*

THE PRIEST PREPARES AND PARTAKES IN THE BODY AND BLOOD AND SHARES THE WORD

They shall not hunger nor thirst; neither shall the heat nor sun smite them: for He that hath mercy on them shall lead them, even by the springs of water shall he guide them. (Isaiah 49:10)

They shall hunger no more, neither thirst any more; neither shall the sun light on them, nor any heat. (Revelation 7:16)

But one of the soldiers with a spear pierced His side, and forthwith came there out Blood and Water. (John 19:34)

Jesus answered and said unto her, Whosoever drinketh of this water shall thirst again: But whosoever drinketh of the Water that I shall give him shall never thirst; but the Water that I shall give him shall be in him a well of water springing up into everlasting life. (John 4:13-14)

Moreover he said unto me, Son of man, eat that thou findest; eat this roll [i.e., scroll], and go speak unto the house of Israel. So I opened my mouth, and he caused me to eat that roll. And he said unto me, son of man, cause thy belly to eat, and fill thy bowels with this roll that I give thee. Then I did eat it; and t was in my mouth as honey for sweetness. (Ezekiel 3:1-3)

APPENDIX A: *The Bible Is the True Source of the Traditional Anglican Mass – A Biblical Sacramental Reference Guide*

Because God is also His Son and the Word, the eating of His Son is also the digesting of the Word, and vice versa.

UNREPENTANT MORTAL SINNERS

> For I have received of the Lord that which also I delivered unto you, that the Lord Jesus the same night in which He was betrayed took bread: And when He had given thanks, He brake it, and said, Take, eat: this is my body, which is broken for you: this do in remembrance of me. After the same manner also He took the cup, when He had supped, saying, this cup is the new testament in my blood: this do ye, as oft as ye drink it, in remembrance of me. For as often as ye eat this bread, and drink this cup, ye do shew the Lord's death till He come. Wherefore whosoever shall eat this bread, and drink this cup of the Lord, unworthily, shall be guilty of the body and blood of the Lord. But let a man examine himself, and so let him eat of that bread, and drink of that cup. For he that eateth and drinketh unworthily, eateth and drinketh damnation to himself, not discerning the Lord's body. (1 Corinthians 11:23-29)

Unrepentant mortal sinners cannot hope to share in Holy Communion. The discerning Priest must guard against this. Bereft of his receipt of their real profession of Faith and sincere thirsting for the Host, they are deemed incapable and unwilling to comprehend the anaphora, *or understand the* epiclesis, *or enjoin in the* anamnesis *of our Eucharistic Eternal Memory. The Host must be refused to them. That priest who fails to do so is guilty of a great crime against Our Lord. He shall be as guilty as Eli the priest, "for the iniquity which he knoweth; because his sons made themselves vile, and he restrained them not" (1 Samuel 3:13).*

THE PRAYER FOR CHRIST'S CHURCH

> All that the Father giveth me shall come to me; and him that cometh to me I will in no wise cast out. (John 6:37)

> Behold, how good and how pleasant it is for brethren to dwell together in unity! It is like the precious ointment upon the head, that ran down upon the beard, even Aaron's beard: that went down to the skirts of his garments; As the dew of Hermon, and as the dew that descended upon the mountains of Zion: for there the Lord commanded the blessing, even life for evermore. (Psalm 133:1-3)

The Prayer for Christ's Church beseeches Christ to write the Law in our hearts; to accept alms and to offer prayers and oblations; and to engender concord, and not division, through the rule of catholic unity and the pursuit of peace.

APPENDIX A: *The Bible Is the True Source of the Traditional Anglican Mass - A Biblical Sacramental Reference Guide*

THE CHURCH, THE BRIDE OF CHRIST, ARISES FROM THE RIB CAGE OF THE SECOND ADAM

> And the Lord God caused a deep sleep to fall upon Adam, and he slept: and he took one of his ribs, and closed up the flesh instead thereof; and the rib, which the Lord God had taken from man, made he a woman, and brought her unto the man . And Adam said, This is now bone of my bones, and flesh of my flesh: she shall be called Woman, because she was taken out of Man. (Genesis 2:21-23)
>
> But one of the soldiers with a spear pierced His Side, and forthwith came there out Blood and Water. (John 19:34)
>
> For we are members of His body, of His flesh, and of His bones. (Ephesians 5:30)

At Jesus's death on the Cross, the Blood and Water that came out of His rib-cage wound is His resultant Church, His Bride. We are water, as of Creation, washed and saved in His Blood, eating of His propitiation for our sins, at the eternally remembered Marriage Supper known as Holy Communion. This Marriage Supper thus sires the fruit of many new believers.

CHRIST CAME NOT TO GIVE EVERYDAY DAILY BREAD BUT RATHER TO BE THE BREAD OF LIFE

> The sweat of thy face shalt thou eat bread, till thou return unto the ground; for out of it wast thou taken: for dust thou art, and unto

APPENDIX A: The Bible Is the True Source of the Traditional Anglican Mass – A Biblical Sacramental Reference Guide

> dust shalt thou return. And the Lord God said, Behold, the man is become as one of us, to know good and evil: and now, lest He put forth His hand, and take also of the tree of life, and eat, and live forever. (Genesis 3:19,22)

> Labour not for the meat which perisheth, but for that meat which endureth unto everlasting life, which the Son of man shall give unto you: for Him hath God the Father sealed. (John 6:27)

> But he answered [Satan] and said, It is written, Man shall not live by bread alone, but by every word that proceedeth out of the mouth of God. (Matthew 4:4)

THE FREE GIFT OF GRACE WORKS MORE ABUNDANTLY THROUGH CHRISTIANS THAN SIN AND DOUBT DO

> Nevertheless death reigned from Adam to Moses, even over them that had not sinned after the similitude of Adam's transgression, who is the figure of Him that was to come. But not as the offence, so also is the free gift. For if through the offence of one many be dead, much more the grace of God, and the gift by grace, which is by one man, Jesus Christ, hath abounded unto many. (Romans 5:14-15)

APPENDIX A: The Bible Is the True Source of the Traditional Anglican Mass – A Biblical Sacramental Reference Guide

OLD-TESTAMENT SOURCES OF RITUAL BREAD

And thou shalt set upon the table shewbread before me alway. (Exodus 25:30)

And thou shalt take fine flour, and bake twelve cakes thereof: two tenth deals shall be in one cake. And thou shalt set them in two rows, six on a row, upon the pure table before the Lord. And thou shalt put pure frankincense upon each row, that it may be on the bread for a memorial, even an offering made by fire unto the Lord. (Leviticus 24:5-7)

And upon the table of shewbread they shall spread a cloth of blue, and put thereon the dishes, and the spoons, and the bowls, and covers to cover withal: and the continual bread shall be thereon. (Numbers 4:7)

WELCOMING TO THE FEASTS THAT REFLECT CONGREGANTS' FAITH IN ETERNAL LIFE

The meek shall eat and be satisfied: they shall praise the Lord that seek Him: your heart shall live for ever. All they that be fat upon earth shall eat and worship: all they that go down to the dust shall bow before Him: and none can keep alive His own soul. (Psalm 22:26,29)

Come, eat of my bread, and drink of the wine which I have mingled. (Proverbs 9:5)

APPENDIX A: The Bible Is the True Source of the Traditional Anglican Mass - A Biblical Sacramental Reference Guide

I am come into my garden, my sister, my spouse: I have gathered my myrrh with my spice; I have eaten my honeycomb with my honey; I have drunk my wine with my milk: eat, O friends; drink, yea, drink abundantly, O beloved. (Song of Solomon 5:1)

And in this mountain shall the Lord of hosts make unto all people a feast of fat things, a feast of wines on the lees, of fat things full of marrow, of wines on the lees well refined. (Isaiah 25:6)

And did all eat the same spiritual meat; And did all drink the same spiritual drink: for they drank of that spiritual Rock that followed them: and that Rock was Christ. (1 Corinthians 10:3-4)

And this day shall be unto you for a memorial; and ye shall keep it a feast to the Lord throughout your generations; ye shall keep it a feast by an ordinance for ever. (Exodus 12:14)

HOLY COMMUNION RENEWS THE PASSOVER FEAST UNDER THE NEW COVENANT OF GRACE

Then Joshua called the twelve men, whom he had prepared of the children of Israel, out of every tribe a man: And Joshua said unto them, Pass over before the ark of the Lord your God into the midst of Jordan, and take you up every man of you a stone upon his shoulder, according unto the number of the

APPENDIX A: The Bible Is the True Source of the Traditional Anglican Mass - A Biblical Sacramental Reference Guide

tribes of the children of Israel: That this may be a sign among you, that when your children ask their fathers in time to come, saying, What mean ye by these stones? Then ye shall answer them, That the waters of Jordan were cut off before the ark of the covenant of the Lord; when it passed over Jordan, the waters of Jordan were cut off: and these stones shall be for a memorial unto the children of Israel for ever ... And the people came up out of Jordan on the tenth day of the first month, and encamped in Gilgal, in the east border of Jericho. That all the people of the earth might know the hand of the Lord, that it is mighty: that ye might fear the Lord your God for ever. (Joshua 4:4-7,24)

Purge out the old leaven, that ye may be a new lump, as ye are unleavened. For even Christ our passover is sacrificed for us. (1 Corinthians 5:7)

Passover celebrated Israel's escape from Egypt by all Twelve Tribes. Passover began on the tenth day of the first month. Lambs were selected for sacrifice and kept in the home until the fourteenth day of the first month (Exodus 12:2-6).

The Hebrew patriarchs and priests are exchanged today with Christian priests, who orient the Sunday Holy Communion, each "stone" being the very Rock of Faith upon which each church was founded by the Twelve Apostles. In fact, it was for this Rock that Peter was named; Peter was not himself the "Rock" (Matthew 16:18).

APPENDIX A: *The Bible Is the True Source of the Traditional Anglican Mass - A Biblical Sacramental Reference Guide*

MOSES FOUNDED THE LEVITICAL PRIESTHOOD THROUGH AARON AND HIS SONS

> And it came to pass on the eighth day, that Moses called Aaron and his sons, and the elders of Israel; And he said unto Aaron, Take thee a young calf for a sin offering, and a ram for a burnt offering, without blemish, and offer them before the Lord. And Moses said unto Aaron, Go unto the altar, and offer thy sin offering, and thy burnt offering, and make an atonement for thyself, and for the people: and offer the offering of the people, and make an atonement for them; as the Lord commanded. (Leviticus 9:1-2,7)

MODEST ANGLICAN PRIESTLY VESTMENTS PROJECT THE SIMPLE TRUTH OF LOGOS

> Fasten both stones onto the shoulder pieces of the ephod as memorial stones for the sons of Israel. Aaron is to bear their names on his two shoulders as a memorial before the Lord. (Exodus 28:12)

> > The [above] verse is interpreted as signifying Aaron's presentation of the sons of Israel to the Lord, his intercession for them, and his patient bearing of all their infirmities and weaknesses. (John Gill, *Exposition of the Entire Bible*, 1748-1763).

> > [The priestly breastplate, the Ephod] was composed of folded cloth, in which were

APPENDIX A: *The Bible Is the True Source of the Traditional Anglican Mass - A Biblical Sacramental Reference Guide*

> lodged twelve precious stones, in four rows of three, each stone containing the name of one of the tribes. It was held in position by the ephod, which consisted of another piece of cloth, with a back and front part, which were united into one on the shoulders. On each shoulder it was clasped by an onyx stone bearing the names of six of the tribes. Thus twice, on the shoulders, the seat of power, and on the heart, the organ of thought and of love, Aaron, entering into the presence of the Most High, bore "the names of the tribes for a memorial continually."
> (Alexander MacLaren, *Expositions of Holy Scripture*, 1904)

And thou shalt put in the breastplate of judgment the Urim and the Thummim; and they shall be upon Aaron's heart, when he goeth in before the Lord: and Aaron shall bear the judgment of the children of Israel upon his heart before the Lord continually. (Exodus 28:30)

Though austerely appointed, the Ephod and the breastplate, could not repel the horrible sins that led to the destruction of Israel in A.D. 70 any more than the breakdown of society that is caused by Moral Relativism and Dialectic Materialism (etc.) threatens to annihilate modern America. Only Christ saves. Not the priestly vestments or the Law. The sins of Modernism stem from the refusal to accept Truth that God is One. The spirits of Eros, Vanity, Avarice, and

APPENDIX A: The Bible Is the True Source of the Traditional Anglican Mass - A Biblical Sacramental Reference Guide

Variance or Faction cause unrest and division that must be removed by the clergy (Galatians 5:19-23). All aspects of the priesthood must exemplify the Absolute Truth and Objective Morality of God, together with the simple conservative presence of the patriarch at all times.

The Urim and the Thummim were never intended to be means of cleromancy (the casting of lots). They were miraculous devices to help a priest explain how God means Scripture to concern the worshipper. That is, visual reflections upon rays of the Sun, or of a torch, used to cause one of either of these gemstones to produce a certain glow, which functioned as the answering of, a "yes" or "no" to a question posed to the synagogue priest by the visitor. He was hoped to interpret the miraculous light occurring through these stones, but not to invoke divine "sortition" as if he could summon forward the presumed randomness that supplicants could hope may be dispensed upon them by God in their favor. In those times, a different God-dispensed era indeed, these stones were miraculous articles connected to God, rather than being tiny slot machines (1 Samuel 14:41; 1 Samuel 10:22; 2 Samuel 5:23). Moreover, the word, "luck," is rightly nowhere in the King James Bible. God gave the Word and the Urim and Thummim as means of employing Faith, not for sinful wagering as to what He has in mind for each person.

> But let patience have her perfect work, that ye may be perfect and entire, wanting

APPENDIX A: *The Bible Is the True Source of the Traditional Anglican Mass - A Biblical Sacramental Reference Guide*

> nothing. If any of you lack wisdom, let him ask of God, that giveth to all men liberally, and upbraideth not; and it shall be given him. But let him ask in Faith, nothing wavering. For he that wavereth is like a wave of the sea driven with the wind and tossed. For let not that man think that he shall receive any thing of the Lord. (James 1:4-7)

Misunderstanding the Ephod's purpose, as though used for the priest's arbitrary determining of Truth, would have more in common with pagan aesthetics than with the Absolute Truth of God. Socrates had said to the mathematician: "So neither perception, Theaetetus, nor true opinion, nor reason or explanation combined with true opinion could be knowledge" (Plato, Theaetetus; *Part 210:a-b; B.C. 360). Wrong indeed! Knowing the truth of the Bible, the Word of God, will instead set us free (John 8:32). Priests must confront this permanent battle, as Pontius Pilate had quipped: What is Truth? (John 18:38).*

At all times, reality must instead be confessed through the Logos, the Truth Who is Christ, so that there is never any question about justified true belief. "But let your communication be, Yea, yea; Nay, nay: for whatsoever is more than these cometh of evil" (Matthew 5:37).

Anglican vestments are simple, but they represent the Order, Office, and Function of the minister.

APPENDIX A: The Bible Is the True Source of the Traditional Anglican Mass - A Biblical Sacramental Reference Guide

A black Cassock is worn underneath a white Surplice, over which a stole hangs vertically over both shoulders of the Priest and diagonally over the left shoulder of the ordained Deacon or appointed Deaconess. When he is apart from the altar, perhaps to teach, give a speech, or preach, the priest may wear a plain Tippet.

The Stole and Tippet always bear the flat Liturgical color of the day and/or period, as does the Chasuble that is worn by the Priest. The Chasuble, symbolizing Christ's seamless garment, is worn over his Cassock and underneath his plain white Alb, in lieu of the Surplice.

The Priest wears the Cassock, Surplice, and Stole during the Daily Office, regular masses, and during any other liturgical moment. He wears the Cassock, Stole, Alb, and Chasuble during higher holy days, such as Easter, Trinity Sunday, Christmas, the Allhallowtide Triduum, etc., and for sacraments such as ordinations, consecrations, and Holy Baptism. He wraps a thick rope known as a Cincture around his Alb and tucks his stole to form an X beneath his Cincture.

> And thou shalt put the mitre upon his head, and put the holy crown upon the mitre. (Exodus 29:6)

Bishops and Archbishops may wear all of the above, for all of the above reasons. But they uniquely wear the Mitre, behind which two fringed lappets hang.

APPENDIX A: The Bible Is the True Source of the Traditional Anglican Mass – A Biblical Sacramental Reference Guide

The Mitres of the Anglo-Catholics and the Eastern Orthodox sometimes are bulb-shaped, as if they are wise-man crowns. (As a side note, the Roman Catholic Church, until 2013, alternated the Mitre with the wearing of a sacerdotal jeweled Tiara).

Bishops may also wear Medieval garments known as a Cope and a Humeral Veil, which respectively resemble a cape and shawl. The Mitre, Cope, and Humeral Veil are colored for the day and/or liturgical season, and are worn at higher holy days, for the sacraments, and at synods.

A Bishop, a Canon, or a Dean of the Church may, for academic conferences or synods, wear a sleeveless black academic gown known as a Chimere. It is worn over the white Alb in place of the Stole or Tippet. Instead of the Alb, he can wear the Chimere with a white choir robe, or the lusher white Rochet, and can opt for wearing wrist bands. He may, during synods, lectures, important meetings, public appearances, or speeches, wear the Rochet with a three-pointed "Canterbury cap" or Biretta on his head. The stole, the Chimere, the Tippet, and the wrist bands are usually all black, but otherwise the same liturgical color must be uniformly reflected by each item.

The traditional colors of the Cassock per minister are as follows: Deacons/Deaconesses wear grey. Priests wear black. Canons wear blue. Bishops wear purple. The Archbishop wears blood or scarlet red. Ordained ministers may wear "dog" or tabbed collars.

APPENDIX A: The Bible Is the True Source of the Traditional Anglican Mass - A Biblical Sacramental Reference Guide

The canons and the bishops may wear a long black Cassock with 33 red buttons (or 39 to emblemize the 39 Articles). The Cassock may also have fewer buttons and/or be thigh- or waist-length. The Cassock may be paired with a blood- or scarlet-red Fascia or Cincture, wrapped or tied around the waist.

JESUS IS THE HIGH PRIEST — THE TABERNACLE AND THE LAW

> But Christ being come an high priest of good things to come, by a greater and more perfect tabernacle, not made with hands, that is to say, not of this building; Neither by the blood of goats and calves, but by his own blood he entered in once into the holy place, having obtained eternal redemption for us. (Hebrews 9:11-12)
>
> And the Word was made flesh, and dwelt among us, (and we beheld His glory, the glory as of the only begotten of the Father,) full of Grace and Truth. (John 1:14)
>
> Jesus answered and said unto them, Destroy this temple, and in three days I will raise it up. (John 2:19)

CHRIST'S PRIESTHOOD STEMS THROUGH MELCHIZADEK AND AARON

> And Melchizedek king of Salem brought forth bread and wine: and he was the priest of the most high God. And he blessed him,

APPENDIX A: The Bible Is the True Source of the Traditional Anglican Mass – A Biblical Sacramental Reference Guide

> and said, Blessed be Abram of the most high God, possessor of Heaven and earth: And blessed be the most high God, Which hath delivered thine enemies into thy hand. And [Abram] gave him tithes of all. (Genesis 14:18-20)

> The LORD said unto my Lord, Sit thou at my right hand, until I make thine enemies thy footstool... The Lord hath sworn, and will not repent, Thou art a priest forever after the order of Melchizedek. (Psalm 110:1,4)

The Psalmist speaks directly of the Messiah and about an eternal priesthood. If such a priest could summon the salvific benevolence of the Father and destroy the wicked (as the Psalms constantly request), then who would be this mystical, eternal Priest if not Christ Himself? Thus, through the institution of the priesthood by Christ at the Last Supper, all Christian priests descend from this eternal Order.

> For this Melchizedek, king of Salem, priest of the most high God, who met Abraham returning from the slaughter of the kings, and blessed him; To whom also Abraham gave a tenth part of all; first being by interpretation King of righteousness, and after that also King of Salem, which is, King of peace; Without father, without mother, without descent, having neither beginning of days, nor end of life; but made like unto the Son of God; abideth a priest continually. Now consider how great this man was, unto whom

APPENDIX A: *The Bible Is the True Source of the Traditional Anglican Mass – A Biblical Sacramental Reference Guide*

even the patriarch Abraham gave the tenth of the spoils. And verily they that are of the sons of Levi, who receive the office of the priesthood, have a commandment to take tithes of the people according to the law, that is, of their brethren, though they come out of the loins of Abraham: But he whose descent is not counted from them received tithes of Abraham, and blessed him that had the promises. And without all contradiction the less is blessed of the better. And here men that die receive tithes; but there he receiveth them, of whom it is witnessed that he liveth. And as I may so say, Levi also, who receiveth tithes, payed tithes in Abraham. For he was yet in the loins of his father, when Melchizedek met him. If therefore perfection were by the Levitical priesthood, (for under it the people received the law,) what further need was there that another priest should rise after the order of Melchizedek, and not be called after the order of Aaron? For the priesthood being changed, there is made of necessity a change also of the law. For he of whom these things are spoken pertaineth to another tribe, of which no man gave attendance at the altar. For it is evident that our Lord sprang out of Juda; of which tribe Moses spake nothing concerning priesthood. And it is yet far more evident: for that after the similitude of Melchizedek there ariseth another priest, Who is made, not after the law of a carnal commandment, but after the power of an endless life. For he testifieth, Thou art a priest for ever after the order of

APPENDIX A: The Bible Is the True Source of the Traditional Anglican Mass - A Biblical Sacramental Reference Guide

Melchizedek. For there is verily a disannulling of the commandment going before for the weakness and unprofitableness thereof. For the law made nothing perfect, but the bringing in of a better hope did; by the which we draw nigh unto God. And inasmuch as not without an oath he was made priest (For those priests were made without an oath; but this with an oath by Him that said unto him, The Lord sware and will not repent, Thou art a priest for ever after the order of Melchizedek:) By so much was Jesus made a surety of a better testament. And they truly were many priests, because they were not suffered to continue by reason of death: But this man, because he continueth ever, hath an unchangeable priesthood. Wherefore he is able also to save them to the uttermost that come unto God by him, seeing he ever liveth to make intercession for them. For such an high priest became us, who is holy, harmless, undefiled, separate from sinners, and made higher than the heavens; Who needeth not daily, as those high priests, to offer up sacrifice, first for his own sins, and then for the people's: for this he did once, when he offered up himself. For the law maketh men high priests which have infirmity; but the word of the oath, which was since the law, maketh the Son, who is consecrated for evermore. (Hebrews 7:1-28)

APPENDIX A: The Bible Is the True Source of the Traditional Anglican Mass – A Biblical Sacramental Reference Guide

THANKSGIVING: PRAYED BY BOTH PRIEST AND CONGREGATION IN GLAD FELLOWSHIP

He hath made his wonderful works to be remembered: the Lord is gracious and full of compassion. (Psalm 111:4)

Draw me, we will run after thee: the king hath brought me into his chambers: we will be glad and rejoice in thee, we will remember thy love more than wine: the upright love thee. (Song of Solomon 1:4)

Yea, in the way of thy judgments, O Lord, have we waited for thee; the desire of our soul is to thy name, and to the remembrance of thee. (Isaiah 26:8)

For in that she hath poured this ointment on my body, she did it for my burial. Verily I say unto you, Wheresoever this Gospel shall be preached in the whole world, there shall also this, that this woman hath done, be told for a memorial of her. (Matthew 26:12-13)

SURSUM CORDA — THE PREFACE TO THE *ANAPHORA* OF OUR APOSTOLIC TRADITION

Let us lift up our heart with our hands unto God in the heavens. (Lamentations 3:41)

Lift up your heads, O ye gates; and be ye lift up, ye everlasting doors; and the King of glory shall come in. Who is this King of glory? The Lord strong and mighty, the Lord mighty

APPENDIX A: The Bible Is the True Source of the Traditional Anglican Mass – A Biblical Sacramental Reference Guide

in battle. Lift up your heads, O ye gates; even lift them up, ye everlasting doors; and the King of glory shall come in. Who is this King of glory? The Lord of hosts, He is the King of glory. Selah. (Psalm 24:7-10)

THE SANCTUS ("HOLY, HOLY, HOLY"): CONSIDERING THE CHURCH WHERE IT IS PRAYED

In the year that King Uzziah died I saw also the Lord sitting upon a throne, high and lifted up, and His train filled the temple. Above it stood the seraphims: each one had six wings; with twain He covered His face, and with twain He covered His feet, and with twain he did fly. And one cried unto another, and said, Holy, holy, holy, is the Lord of hosts: the whole earth is full of His glory. And the posts of the door moved at the voice of Him that cried, and the house was filled with smoke. Then said I, Woe is me! for I am undone; because I am a man of unclean lips, and I dwell in the midst of a people of unclean lips: for mine eyes have seen the King, the Lord of hosts. (Isaiah 6:1-5)

For I am the Lord your God: ye shall therefore sanctify yourselves, and ye shall be holy; for I am holy: neither shall ye defile yourselves with any manner of creeping thing that creepeth upon the earth. (Leviticus 11:44)

APPENDIX A: The Bible Is the True Source of the Traditional Anglican Mass - A Biblical Sacramental Reference Guide

COMMUNION ADVANCING *THEOSIS* WITH THE RISEN AND ASCENDED LORD

And for this cause He is the mediator of the new testament, that by means of death, for the redemption of the transgressions that were under the first testament, they which are called might receive the promise of eternal inheritance. For a testament is of force after men are dead: otherwise it is of no strength at all while the testator liveth. Whereupon neither the first testament was dedicated without blood. For when Moses had spoken every precept to all the people according to the law, he took the blood of calves and of goats, with water, and scarlet wool, and hyssop, and sprinkled both the book, and all the people, Saying, This is the blood of the testament which God hath enjoined unto you. Moreover he sprinkled with blood both the tabernacle, and all the vessels of the ministry. And almost all things are by the law purged with blood; and without shedding of blood is no remission. It was therefore necessary that the patterns of things in the heavens should be purified with these; but the heavenly things themselves with better sacrifices than these. For Christ is not entered into the holy places made with hands, which are the figures of the true; but into heaven itself, now to appear in the presence of God for us: Nor yet that he should offer himself often, as the high priest entereth into the holy place every year with blood of others; For then must he often have

APPENDIX A: The Bible Is the True Source of the Traditional Anglican Mass - A Biblical Sacramental Reference Guide

> suffered since the foundation of the world: but now once in the end of the world hath he appeared to put away sin by the sacrifice of himself. And as it is appointed unto men once to die, but after this the judgment: So Christ was once offered to bear the sins of many; and unto them that look for him shall he appear the second time without sin unto salvation. (Hebrews 9:15-28)

In that Eternal Memory is itself the New Testament and Revelation of the Lord, Jesus by His death and Resurrection has left a Last Will and Testament to be followed, by our celebrating of the Mass and living upright Christian lives until we are granted ultimate Salvation.

THEOSIS: AT THE TIME OF SALVATION, THE SAVED SHALL COMPLETELY BECOME ONE AND REUNITED WITH GOD

> Beloved, now we are the sons of God, and it doth not yet appear what we shall be: but we know that, when He shall appear, we shall be like Him; for we shall see Him as He is. (1 John 3:2)

> Neither pray I for these alone, but for them also which shall believe on me through their word; That they all may be one; as thou, Father, art in me, and I in thee, that they also may be one in us: that the world may believe that thou hast sent me. And the glory which thou gavest me I have given them; that they may be one, even as we are one: I in them,

APPENDIX A: The Bible Is the True Source of the Traditional Anglican Mass – A Biblical Sacramental Reference Guide

and thou in me, that they may be made perfect in one; and that the world may know that thou hast sent me, and hast loved them, as thou hast loved me. (John 17:20-23)

I have said, Ye are gods; and all of you are children of the most High. (Psalm 82:6)

Jesus answered them, Is it not written in your law, I said, Ye are gods? (John 10:34)

The Apostolic Fathers reiterated these biblical truths and stressed the vital importance of theosis *as the ultimate end of the Christian Faith: "The Son of God became man, that we might become god" [or, "becoming by grace what God is by nature"] (St. Athanasius,* De Incarnatione de Verbi; *Part 54; Section 3; A.D. ~320). And again: [T]he Word of God, our Lord Jesus Christ ... did, through His transcendent love, become what we are, that He might bring us to be even what He is Himself" (St. Irenaeus,* Adversus Haereses; *Book V; Pref.; A.D. 180).*

PRAYER AND CONTEMPLATION BEYOND THE CHURCH WALLS AND HEARD BY GOD

Be careful for nothing; but in every thing by prayer and supplication with thanksgiving let your requests be made known unto God. (Philippians 4:6)

And in that day ye shall ask me nothing. Verily, verily, I say unto you, Whatsoever ye shall ask the Father in my name, he will give

APPENDIX A: The Bible Is the True Source of the Traditional Anglican Mass - A Biblical Sacramental Reference Guide

it you. Hitherto have ye asked nothing in my name: ask, and ye shall receive, that your joy may be full. (John 16:23-24)

Beloved, believe not every spirit, but try the spirits whether they are of God: because many false prophets are gone out into the world. (1 John 4:1)

Examine yourselves, whether ye be in the faith; prove your own selves. Know ye not your own selves, how that Jesus Christ is in you, except ye be reprobates? (2 Corinthians 13:5)

But thou, when thou prayest, enter into thy closet, and when thou hast shut thy door, pray to thy Father which is in secret; and thy Father which seeth in secret shall reward thee openly. (Matthew 6:6)

Pray without ceasing. (1 Thessalonians 5:17)

Neglect not the gift that is in thee, which was given thee by prophecy, with the laying on of the hands of the presbytery. Meditate upon these things; give thyself wholly to them; that thy profiting may appear to all. Take heed unto thyself, and unto the doctrine; continue in them: for in doing this thou shalt both save thyself, and them that hear thee. (1 Timothy 4:14-16)

APPENDIX A: The Bible Is the True Source of the Traditional Anglican Mass - A Biblical Sacramental Reference Guide

COLLECT FOR PURITY

Thus shall Aaron come into the holy place: with a young bullock for a sin offering, and a ram for a burnt offering. He shall put on the holy linen coat, and he shall have the linen breeches upon his flesh, and shall be girded with a linen girdle, and with the linen mitre shall he be attired: these are holy garments; therefore shall he wash his flesh in water, and so put them on. (Leviticus 16:3-4)

Let no man despise thy youth; but be thou an example of the believers, in word, in conversation, in charity, in spirit, in faith, in purity. (1 Timothy 4:12)

Finally, brethren, whatsoever things are true, whatsoever things are honest, whatsoever things are just, whatsoever things are pure, whatsoever things are lovely, whatsoever things are of good report; if there be any virtue, and if there be any praise, think on these things. (Philippians 4:8)

CONFESSION, ABSOLUTION, AND REMISSION OF SINS

And see if there be any wicked way in me, and lead me in the way everlasting. (Psalm 139:23-24)

Create in me a clean heart, O God; and renew a right spirit within me. Cast me not away from thy presence; and take not thy holy

APPENDIX A: The Bible Is the True Source of the Traditional Anglican Mass – A Biblical Sacramental Reference Guide

spirit from me. Restore unto me the joy of thy salvation; and uphold me with thy free spirit. Then will I teach transgressors thy ways; and sinners shall be converted unto thee. Deliver me from bloodguiltiness, O God, thou God of my salvation: and my tongue shall sing aloud of thy righteousness. O Lord, open thou my lips; and my mouth shall shew forth thy praise. For thou desirest not sacrifice; else would I give it: thou delightest not in burnt offering. The sacrifices of God are a broken spirit: a broken and a contrite heart, O God, thou wilt not despise. Do good in thy good pleasure unto Zion: build thou the walls of Jerusalem. Then shalt thou be pleased with the sacrifices of righteousness, with burnt offering and whole burnt offering: then shall they offer bullocks upon thine altar. (Psalm 51:10-19)

HOMILIES: "AND SUCH WERE SOME OF YOU"

Know ye not that the unrighteous shall not inherit the kingdom of God? Be not deceived: neither fornicators, nor idolaters, nor adulterers, nor effeminate, nor abusers of themselves with mankind, Nor thieves, nor covetous, nor drunkards, nor revilers, nor extortioners, shall inherit the kingdom of God. And such were some of you: but ye are washed, but ye are sanctified, but ye are justified in the name of the Lord Jesus, and by the Spirit of our God. (Corinthians 6:9-11)

APPENDIX A: The Bible Is the True Source of the Traditional Anglican Mass - A Biblical Sacramental Reference Guide

As described earlier in this book, the expression "Holy things are for the Holy" originated in the Catechetical Lectures *of Saint Cyril of Jerusalem, just as it appeared in subsequent liturgies (such as that of Saint Basil). It calls orthodox Christian believers to take their exclusive place at the Communion Rail, and although it is not in the 1928 BCP, it is good to mention it during homilies. Catechized Christians, each of whom have received Baptism, Confirmation, and other sacraments and religious instruction, are perceived to have been taught to retain within themselves the image of God and not to deliberately associate their psyches and bodies with profane and sordid uses of the world, the filth out of which they have been saved. People who relinquish themselves to the unsaved state, the "inhabiters of the ground," will experience the woe of Satan's wrath (Revelation 8:13; 12:12), which cannot even compare to the wrath of God (Revelation 6:12-17). More than those who have never heard the Word, Christians who were long taught Truth but have fallen back like dogs into their own vomit (2 Peter 2:2), or who hide in their unrepentant mortal sin and ignore God's Word, eventually witness their well-swept psyches being beset with additional demons (Matthew 12:38-45), presenting the greater cause for a recurrent reminder that the Eucharist is not given so that an intentionally unholy person can wet her uncommitted beak, or dip his cynical toe, into the water of Salvation only snatch it back again gracelessly. Rather, it is meant for those whom God would likely regard as being sincere imitators of Christ.*

APPENDIX A: *The Bible Is the True Source of the Traditional Anglican Mass - A Biblical Sacramental Reference Guide*

GLORIA IN EXCELSIS: HOW THE BIBLICAL SACRAMENTS GUARD ONE'S PRAYERFUL MIND AGAINST THE CURSES ASSOCIATED WITH ADAM, EVE, THE SERPENT, AND THE LAW OF MOSES

> Unto the woman he said, I will greatly multiply thy sorrow and thy conception; in sorrow thou shalt bring forth children; and thy desire shall be to thy husband, and he shall rule over thee. And unto Adam he said, Because thou hast hearkened unto the voice of thy wife, and hast eaten of the tree, of which I commanded thee, saying, Thou shalt not eat of it: cursed is the ground for thy sake; in sorrow shalt thou eat of it all the days of thy life; Thorns also and thistles shall it bring forth to thee; and thou shalt eat the herb of the field; In the sweat of thy face shalt thou eat bread, till thou return unto the ground; for out of it wast thou taken: for dust thou art, and unto dust shalt thou return. (Genesis 3:16-19)

The Fall of Man in Genesis 3 descended upon humanity through curses—with bad happenstances galore, and the inevitable hardships that make living a peaceful life all but impossible. God cursed Eve to follow Adam, along with all the hardships that the world would set against the human family like a snake. Thus women give birth in severe agony and suffer countless lifelong heartbreaks.

APPENDIX A: The Bible Is the True Source of the Traditional Anglican Mass – A Biblical Sacramental Reference Guide

> Let your women keep silence in the churches: for it is not permitted unto them to speak; but they are commanded to be under obedience as also saith the law. And if they will learn anything, let them ask their husbands at home: for it is a shame for women to speak in the church. (1 Corinthians 14:34-35)

Perhaps as part of this curse, women are not permitted to preside over or preach in churches, and that is because she must always be under the authority of her husband (1 Timothy 2:12; 1 Corinthians 14:34-35). Women, nevertheless, may teach other women (Titus 2:3-5). As the wives of priests and bishops, they may be teachers in winning over their husbands to their chaste counsel inspired by the Lord.

> And the LORD God said unto the woman, What is this that thou hast done? And the woman said, The serpent beguiled me, and I did eat. And the LORD God said unto the serpent, Because thou hast done this, thou art cursed above all cattle, and above every beast of the field; upon thy belly shalt thou go, and dust shalt thou eat all the days of thy life: And I will put enmity between thee and the woman, and between thy seed and her seed; it shall bruise thy head, and thou shalt bruise his heel. (Genesis 3:13-15)

The snake was itself cursed to creep along the ground forever, always thrusting its fangs against mothers and their children for all time. It

APPENDIX A: The Bible Is the True Source of the Traditional Anglican Mass - A Biblical Sacramental Reference Guide

will even murderously chase the Holy Mother, alternately interpreted as the Blessed Mother Mary and the Bride of Christ (the Church), together with her children, through the End of Days (Revelation 12:15-17).

> Because, even because they have seduced my people, saying, Peace; and there was no peace; and one built up a wall, and, lo, others daubed it with un-tempered mortar. (Ezekiel 13:10)

> For unto us a child is born, unto us a son is given: and the government shall be upon His shoulder: and his name shall be called Wonderful, Counsellor, The mighty God, The everlasting Father, the Prince of Peace. (Isaiah 9:6-7)

God cursed Adam and Eve, our first parents, with expulsion from the eternally blessed garden and with lifelong work and woes. He will lose his son Abel to murder, and man will see the fruit of his labor and all sources of his pride turn to dust. But we are assured of the hope of Salvation and the New Jerusalem through Christ our Lord, who is the New Adam and Prince of Peace.

> Glory be to God on high, and on earth peace, good will towards men. We praise Thee, we bless Thee, we worship Thee, we glorify Thee, we give thanks to Thee for Thy great glory, O Lord God, heavenly King, God the Father Almighty. *(Gloria in Excelsis; 1928 Book of Common Prayer)*

APPENDIX A: The Bible Is the True Source of the Traditional Anglican Mass - A Biblical Sacramental Reference Guide

The Eucharist is disbursed to the Faithful in order to endow with Hope the heart of the communicant, who knows by Revelation that as soon as the Comforter is taken out of the way, the world as we know it will end (John 14:16-20; 2 Thessalonians 2:7). He hopes for a real Peace, and not the false peace of white-washed sins.

> Thus saith the Lord, which giveth the sun for a light by day, and the ordinances of the moon and of the stars for a light by night, which divideth the sea when the waves thereof roar; The Lord of hosts is His name: If those ordinances depart from before me, saith the Lord, then the seed of Israel also shall cease from being a nation before me forever. Thus saith the Lord; If heaven above can be measured, and the foundations of the earth searched out beneath, I will also cast off all the seed of Israel for all that they have done, saith the Lord. (Jeremiah 31:35-37)

All celestial and natural law are definitively poised at the ready for the ceasing of the "ordinances"—the physical functions of the Earth, the stars, and the planets, which stop operating as soon as the love of man waxes entirely cold, to welcome the false prophet as the stars fall from the sky (Matthew 24:10-13, 2 Timothy 3:1-5), while many Christians fall away from the Church (1 Timothy 4:1), until the son of perdition comes (2 Thessalonians 2:3)—that man of sin who brings the false peace that concludes with the destruction of the world (Daniel 8:23-25; 9:26-27; 11:36-39).

APPENDIX A: The Bible Is the True Source of the Traditional Anglican Mass – A Biblical Sacramental Reference Guide

When communicants squander their receipt of a Sacrament by seeking shortcuts in life, to deliberately lessen their hardship through sinfulness, they are not facing their accursed existence with faithfulness but instead with age-old deceit, as if to correct the God Who had made them, for being capable of mistakes, or as if God is a liar (1 John 1:10).

Therefore, so that sinners would instead confront very honestly and selflessly every single form of enmity imposed by the "snake," and so that they would strive to overcome these requisite curses with Faith, Moses elevated a brass serpent on a pole.

Moses forced the Israelites, whenever bitten by actual snakes (or victimized by tragedy, disease, or their enemies), to gaze upon the metal reptile with deep respect so that they would let God heal their proud denials and any mutterings against how "unfair" life is, and instead abandon their poisoned intellect to humility (Numbers 21:8-32:19).

Thereafter, the message taught by synagogue priests to Hebrew families hoping to understand better their lots in life was, in the Temple Era, activated by the minster's interpretation of the lights reflected through the Urim and Thummim stones, which sat on his Ephod. It is a curious historical fact.

The Levitical report was always crystal-clear in its empathy: that a miserable hardship would

APPENDIX A: The Bible Is the True Source of the Traditional Anglican Mass - A Biblical Sacramental Reference Guide

indeed surely raze anybody. But it also implied that Heaven's so-called randomness during that God-dispensed era could be interpreted according to the mystical cleromancy which the Rabbi believed was activated via these stones—like a therapist rolling "God's dice" for his desperate audience. Surely, although "luck" is mentioned nowhere in the Bible, indeed "the steps of a good man are ordered by the Lord and He delighteth in his way" (Psalm 37:23).

The "wagerers" were understanding that holy acceptance of one's reliance on God as a born sinner in a fallen world will always evoke a truly blessed twofold solution: 1) sane acceptance of the curse of Adam's Fall for as long as it played out during one's difficult life; and 2) prayerful moral probity throughout one's life under the Law of Moses, in spite of the curse.

Just as the woman was cursed to follow her husband permanently, and just as the snake was cursed to sow evil, so the Law of Moses was written by God to navigate the family away from evil. The Chosen accepted the curses placed upon Adam, Eve, and the serpent by associating themselves with the unavoidable necessity of following the Law under penalty of expulsion from the Temple or death.

But upon the Advent of Jesus, the Covenant of Grace promised rebirth into an entirely new paradigm of liberation from the curse of slavery and ultimate death, which were attached to sin and the Law: Christ today presides over and

APPENDIX A: The Bible Is the True Source of the Traditional Anglican Mass – A Biblical Sacramental Reference Guide

becomes the Law, by which He awards Redemption and Heaven for our Faith.

> And as Moses lifted up the serpent in the wilderness, even so must the Son of man be lifted up. (John 3:14)
>
> And the Lord said unto Moses, Make thee a fiery serpent, and set it upon a pole: and it shall come to pass, that every one that is bitten, when he looketh upon it, shall live. (Numbers 21:8)
>
> And Adam called his wife's name Eve; because she was the mother of all living. Unto Adam also and to his wife did the Lord God make coats of skins, and clothed them. And the Lord God said, Behold, the man is become as one of us, to know good and evil: and now, lest he put forth his hand, and take also of the tree of life, and eat, and live for ever: Therefore the Lord God sent him forth from the garden of Eden, to till the ground from whence he was taken. So he drove out the man; and he placed at the east of the garden of Eden Cherubims, and a flaming sword which turned every way, to keep the way of the tree of life. (Genesis 3:20-24)

Upon the Ascension of Christ and the Pentecost, the role of the Church, which firstly flowed with the water of humanity and the Blood of the Lamb out of the wound of the Second Adam's ribs, became the one to bruise the head of the serpent, even though the serpent tried with all its might

APPENDIX A: The Bible Is the True Source of the Traditional Anglican Mass - A Biblical Sacramental Reference Guide

all during each parishioner's lifetime to bite against her heel. Conceived of differently, the Blessed Mother, who is the New Eve, bruised the head of the serpent by participating in the Incarnation of Our Lord, who put death to death: "O death, where is thy sting? O grave, where is thy victory? The sting of death is sin; and the strength of sin is the law. But thanks be to God, which giveth us the victory through our Lord Jesus Christ" (1 Corinthians 15:55-57).

The narrow way back to Eden (Matthew 7:13-29), ably guarded by cherubim from the evil glances of wicked eyes sent across the gulf between Heaven and Hell (Luke 16:19-31), faces appropriately East—the same direction faced by the baptismal font, pulpit, and communion table in many churches.

MASS CLOSING

> The Peace of God, which passeth all understanding, keep your hearts and minds in the knowledge and love of God, and of his Son Jesus Christ our Lord: And the blessing of God Almighty, the Father, the Son, and the Holy Ghost, be amongst you, and remain with you always. Amen. (Philippians 4:7)

The final benediction of the Traditional Anglican Mass is from an epistle by Saint Paul of Tarsus, which he wrote during his imprisonment in Rome. The Epistle to Philippians is one of the four "prison epistles" by Saint Paul (the other three being Ephesians, Colossians, and Philemon; he

APPENDIX A: The Bible Is the True Source of the Traditional Anglican Mass - A Biblical Sacramental Reference Guide

mentions his bondage in Philippians 1:7,13,17). His letter to the Church of Philippi is affectionate and cheerful despite his physical predicament. This Macedonian church (the location of the church is referred to as "Macedon" in Acts 20:1-3 and in 2 Corinthians 2:13; 7:5) was attended by poor but generous slaves, ex-slaves, and retired military men and their families. Philippi was visited by the Apostle during his second missionary journey, and he returns to it briefly during his third. Even though the writer is in bondage, the epistle teems with his affection for his beloved benefactors. This benediction fittingly ends the Mass because it wishes goodness for the recipients along with the encouragement to maintain orthodox devotion to the Logos, Who is Christ, in the sight of the Triune Godhead.

APPENDIX B: Two Church Fathers Who Wrote About the Eucharist and Ecclesiology

FROM EPISTLES BY SAINT IGNATIUS OF ANTIOCH

Meet together frequently for the worship of God: Take heed, then, often to come together to give thanks to God, and show forth His praise. For when you assemble frequently in the same place, the powers of Satan are destroyed, and the destruction at which he aims is prevented by the unity of your faith. Nothing is more precious than peace, by which all war, both in heaven and earth, is brought to an end. *(Epistle to the Ephesians;* Saint Ignatius of Antioch; Chap. 13; A.D. 107-110)

Have but one Eucharist, etc.: Take heed, then, to have but one Eucharist. For there is one flesh of our Lord Jesus Christ, and one cup to [show forth] the unity of His blood; one altar; as there is one bishop, along with the presbytery and deacons, my fellow-servants: that so, whatsoever you do, you may do it according to [the will of] God. *(Epistle to the Philadelphians;* Saint Ignatius of Antioch; Chap. 4; A.D. 107-110)

Let us stand aloof from such heretics: They abstain from the Eucharist and from prayer, because they confess not the Eucharist to be

APPENDIX B: Two Church Fathers, Who Wrote About the Eucharist and Ecclesiology

the flesh of our Saviour Jesus Christ, which suffered for our sins, and which the Father, of His goodness, raised up again. Those, therefore, who speak against this gift of God, incur death in the midst of their disputes. But it were better for them to treat it with respect, that they also might rise again. It is fitting, therefore, that you should keep aloof from such persons, and not to speak of them either in private or in public, but to give heed to the prophets, and above all, to the Gospel, in which the passion [of Christ] has been revealed to us, and the resurrection has been fully proved. But avoid all divisions, as the beginning of evils. *(Epistle to the Smyrnaeans;* Saint Ignatius of Antioch; Chap. 7; A.D. 110)

Let nothing be done without the bishop: See that you all follow the bishop, even as Jesus Christ does the Father, and the presbytery as you would the apostles; and reverence the deacons, as being the institution of God. Let no man do anything connected with the Church without the bishop. Let that be deemed a proper Eucharist, which is [administered] either by the bishop, or by one to whom he has entrusted it. Wherever the bishop shall appear, there let the multitude [of the people] also be; even as, wherever Jesus Christ is, there is the Catholic Church. It is not lawful without the bishop either to baptize or to celebrate a love-feast; but whatsoever he shall approve of, that is also pleasing to God, so that everything that is done may be secure and valid. *(Ibid,* Chap. 8)

APPENDIX B: Two Church Fathers, Who Wrote About the Eucharist and Ecclesiology

FROM THE *FIRST APOLOGY* OF SAINT JUSTIN MARTYR

Administration of the sacraments: But we, after we have thus washed him who has been convinced and has assented to our teaching, bring him to the place where those who are called brethren are assembled, in order that we may offer hearty prayers in common for ourselves and for the baptized [illuminated] person, and for all others in every place, that we may be counted worthy, now that we have learned the truth, by our works also to be found good citizens and keepers of the commandments, so that we may be saved with an everlasting salvation. Having ended the prayers, we salute one another with a kiss. There is then brought to the president of the brethren bread and a cup of wine mixed with water; and he taking them, gives praise and glory to the Father of the universe, through the name of the Son and of the Holy Ghost, and offers thanks at considerable length for our being counted worthy to receive these things at His hands. And when he has concluded the prayers and thanksgivings, all the people present express their assent by saying Amen. This word Amen answers in the Hebrew language to γένοιτο [so be it]. And when the president has given thanks, and all the people have expressed their assent, those who are called by us deacons give to each of those present to partake of the bread and wine mixed with water over which the thanksgiving was

APPENDIX B: Two Church Fathers, Who Wrote About the Eucharist and Ecclesiology

pronounced, and to those who are absent they carry away a portion. *(First Apology;* Saint Justin Martyr; Chap. 65; A.D. 155-157)

Of the Eucharist: And this food is called among us Εὐχαριστία [the Eucharist], of which no one is allowed to partake but the man who believes that the things which we teach are true, and who has been washed with the washing that is for the remission of sins, and unto regeneration, and who is so living as Christ has enjoined. For not as common bread and common drink do we receive these; but in like manner as Jesus Christ our Saviour, having been made flesh by the Word of God, had both flesh and blood for our salvation, so likewise have we been taught that the food which is blessed by the prayer of His word, and from which our blood and flesh by transmutation are nourished, is the flesh and blood of that Jesus who was made flesh. For the apostles, in the memoirs composed by them, which are called Gospels, have thus delivered unto us what was enjoined upon them; that Jesus took bread, and when He had given thanks, said, This do in remembrance of Me, Luke 22:19 this is My body; and that, after the same manner, having taken the cup and given thanks, He said, This is My blood; and gave it to them alone. Which the wicked devils have imitated in the mysteries of Mithras, commanding the same thing to be done. For, that bread and a cup of water are placed with certain incantations in the mystic rites of one who is being initiated, you either know or can learn. *(ibid, First Apology;* Chap. 66)

Weekly worship of the Christians: And we afterwards continually remind each other of these things. And the wealthy among us help the needy; and we always keep together; and for all things wherewith we are supplied, we bless the Maker of all through His Son Jesus Christ, and through the Holy Ghost. And on the day called Sunday, all who live in cities or in the country gather together to one place, and the memoirs of the apostles or the writings of the prophets are read, as long as time permits; then, when the reader has ceased, the president verbally instructs, and exhorts to the imitation of these good things. Then we all rise together and pray, and, as we before said, when our prayer is ended, bread and wine and water are brought, and the president in like manner offers prayers and thanksgivings, according to his ability, and the people assent, saying Amen; and there is a distribution to each, and a participation of that over which thanks have been given, and to those who are absent a portion is sent by the deacons. And they who are well to do, and willing, give what each thinks fit; and what is collected is deposited with the president, who succours the orphans and widows and those who, through sickness or any other cause, are in want, and those who are in bonds and the strangers sojourning among us, and in a word takes care of all who are in need. But Sunday is the day on which

APPENDIX B: Two Church Fathers, Who Wrote About the Eucharist and Ecclesiology

we all hold our common assembly, because it is the first day on which God, having wrought a change in the darkness and matter, made the world; and Jesus Christ our Saviour on the same day rose from the dead. For He was crucified on the day before that of Saturn (Saturday); and on the day after that of Saturn, which is the day of the Sun, having appeared to His apostles and disciples, He taught them these things, which we have submitted to you also for your consideration. *(ibid, First Apology;* Chap. 67)

www.ingramcontent.com/pod-product-compliance
Lightning Source LLC
Chambersburg PA
CBHW050324010526
44119CB00003B/91